# Switch 1

## Workbook

Nicholas Tims

OXFORD

OXFORD
UNIVERSITY PRESS

Great Clarendon Street, Oxford OX2 6DP

Oxford University Press is a department of the University of Oxford. It furthers the University's objective of excellence in research, scholarship, and education by publishing worldwide in

Oxford New York

Auckland Cape Town Dar es Salaam Hong Kong Karachi Kuala Lumpur Madrid Melbourne Mexico City Nairobi New Delhi Shanghai Taipei Toronto

With offices in

Argentina Austria Brazil Chile Czech Republic France Greece Guatemala Hungary Italy Japan Poland Portugal Singapore South Korea Switzerland Thailand Turkey Ukraine Vietnam

OXFORD and OXFORD ENGLISH are registered trade marks of Oxford University Press in the UK and in certain other countries



First published 2010
2014 2013 2012 2011 2010
10 9 8 7 6 5 4 3 2 1



ISBN: 978 0 19 484878 7

Printed in Spain by Orymu S.A.

ACKNOWLEDGEMENTS

*Illustrations by*: Mattia Cerato pp.9, 18, 27 (Ex 1), 30 (Ex 3), 36 (Ex 2); Paul Daviz pp.15, 21, 24 (Ex 2), 39, 42, 48; Kev Hopgood pp.12, 24 (Ex 1), 29, 33, 45; Chris Pavely pp.7, 27 (Ex 2, 3 and 4), 30 (Ex 2), 36 (Ex 1), 54, 60, 85, 97; David Semple pp.91, 95, 101

*We would also like to thank the following for permission to reproduce the following photographs*: Alamy pp.4 (chair/LJSphotography), 4 (pencil case/Rightdisc), 13 (c/RubberBall), 18 (water polo/Trevor Pearson), 18 (ice skating/Koji Aoki/Aflo Foto Agency), 18 (hockey/Colin Underhill), 18 (volleyball/Daniel Dillon), 19 (Chase Jarvis/Corbis Super RF), 25 (Leah Warkentin/Design Pics Inc.), 31 (Manchester/Andrew Fox), 31 (New York/Photogenix), 31 (Sydney/David Wall), 40 (CoverSpot), 42 (strawberries/Shoosh/Form Advertising), 42 (chips/studiomode), 42 (fish/Keith Leighton), 42 (rice/D. Hurst), 43 (Lars/superclic), 51 (7/Somos Images), 51 (8/Oliver Benn), 57 (passport/RoChatterson/Corbis Premium RF), 57 (tent/D. Hurst), 57 (sleeping bag/bobo), 57 (map/Digifoto Sapphire), 86 (Jim West), 92 (Ace Stock Limited), 96 (D. Burke), 100 (Juice Images); Corbis pp.18 (gymnastics/Kevin Dodge), 51 (3/A3817 Tobias Hase/dpa), 51 (11/Michael Ochs Archives), 98 (McPherson Colin/Corbis Sygma); Getty Images pp.4 (desk/Ryan McVay/Photodisc), 8 (Image Source), 10 (Stockbyte), 13 (b/Allison Michael Orenstein/Photodisc), 23 (John Cumming/Digital Vision), 32 (Sami Sarkis/Photographer's Choice), 34 (John Cumming/Iconica), 35 (Flying Colours Ltd/Photodisc), 37 (teenage girls/Dana Neely/Taxi), 37 (cat/Toby Maudsley/Iconica), 37 (teenage boy/Philip and Karen SmithIconica), 43 (Akane/Matt Henry Gunther/Taxi Japan), 43 (Pascal/Jeff Cadge/Photographer's Choice), 46 (Aleksandra Gajdeczka/Flickr), 47 (Stockbyte), 49 (pyramid stage/Tabatha Fireman/Redferns), 49 (guitarist/Christie Goodwin/Redferns), 51 (1/Digital Vision), 51 (6/Kevin Winter), 51 (9/Gary Miller/FilmMagic), 51 (10/David Redfern/Redferns), 57 (towel/Stockbyte), 57 (swimsuit/C Squared Studios/Photodisc), 58 (Fred Paul/Photographer's Choice), 61 (Skip Nall/Digital Vision), 84 (Loungepark/The Image Bank), 90 (Dave Hamman/Gallo Images), 94 (Lew Robertson/Brand X Pictures); iStockphoto.com pp.4 (ruler/DNY59), 13 (a/Sherwin McGehee), 14 (family/Kevin Russ), 16 (Juanmonino), 41 (eggs/Mark Gillow), 54 (violin/Tomaz Levstek), 54 (cello/futureimage), 54 (drums/pixhook), 54 (harp/dvs71), 99 (cymbals/MartinaM); Press Association Images pp.49 (tents/Anthony Devlin/PA Wire), 51 (12/Barry Batchelor/PA Wire); Photolibrary.com pp.57 (box of matches/Ingram Publishing), 88 (Stockbroker/Monkey Business Images Ltd); Rex Features pp.51 (2/Charles Sykes), 51 (4/William T. Wade Jr), 51 (5/Sipa Press), 53 (Brian Rasic), 55 (Johnny Cash/ITV), 55 (The Beatles/KEYSTONE USA), 55 (Bob Marley/Jonathan Player); Royalty-free pp.4 (notebook/Mark Mason), 4 (rubber/Dennis Kitchen Studio, Inc.), 14 (pencil), 14 (ruler), 14 (notebook), 18 (aerobics/Photodisc), 20 (Ingram), 41 (jam/John Foxx), 42 (hamburgers/Ingram), 42 (carrots/Ingram), 42 (sandwiches), 42 (chicken), 54 (guitar/music Alan King), 54 (triangle/Ingram), 54 (trombone/Ingram), 54 (trumpet/Photodisc), 57 (camera/Heather Gail Delaney), 62 (Photodisc), 99 (saxophone/Ingram), 99 (guitar/music Alan King), 99 (trumpet/C Squared Studios/Photodisc)

# Contents


| | | page |
|---|---|---|
| Welcome | | 4 |
| Unit 1 | Look at me! | 9 |
| Unit 2 | At the weekend | 15 |
| Unit 3 | Time for school | 21 |
| Unit 4 | Put on your coat! | 27 |
| Unit 5 | At home | 33 |
| Unit 6 | Are you hungry? | 39 |
| Unit 7 | Cities and towns | 45 |
| Unit 8 | Great music | 51 |
| Unit 9 | Around the world | 57 |
| Grammar Bank | | 63 |
| Vocabulary Bank | | 84 |
| Writing Builder | | 102 |
| Pronunciation Bank | | 111 |
| Word Bank | | 114 |
| Expression Bank | | 120 |
| Irregular Verbs | | 121 |

# Welcome

## Vocabulary

### Numbers 1–20

**1** ★ **Match the numbers and the words.**

| | |
|---|---|
| 4 | ten |
| 10 | twenty |
| 15 | six |
| 6 | four |
| 20 | fifteen |

**2** ★★ **Write the numbers.**

| | | | |
|---|---|---|---|
| 1 | *one* | 5 | five |
| 11 | eleven | 9 | nine |
| 3 | three | 13 | thirteen |

### Colours

**3** ★ **Find seven more colours.**

| | | | | | | | | |
|---|---|---|---|---|---|---|---|---|
| D | T | O | W | H | I | T | E | Q |
| B | Y | T | R | Z | F | N | T | P |
| L | F | B | V | A | R | M | R | M |
| T | F | Y | L | M | N | Q | E | P |
| N | B | M | E | U | B | G | D | R |
| W | R | G | F | L | E | M | E | W |
| K | O | W | J | B | L | A | C | K |
| X | W | J | T | T | P | O | W | R |
| M | N | G | R | E | E | N | W | T |

**4** ★★★ **Write true answers.**

What colour … is the sky? *Blue*

1 … are taxis in your town? Students' answers

2 … is your pencil case? ___________

3 … is your desk? ___________

4 … is your bag? ___________

### Classroom objects

**5** ★★ **Complete the words.**

*ruler*

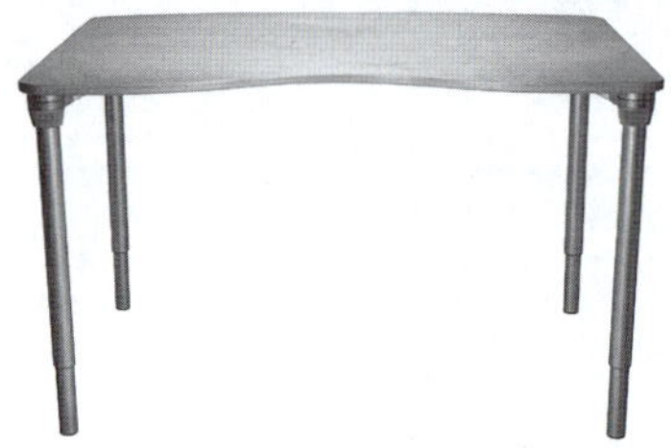

1 d e s k

2 n o t e b o o k

3 c h a i r

4 p e n c i l c a s e

5 r u b b e r

**6** ★★★ **Write true answers.**

What is *Switch*?

*A book.*

1 What's in your pencil case?

Students' answers

2 What's in your school bag?

___________

3 What's on your desk?

___________

## *a / an*

**7** ★★ **Write *a* or *an*.**

an elephant

1 a book

2 a yellow bag

3 an English exam

4 an orange umbrella

5 a maths exam

## Numbers 21–100

**8** ★★ **Write the numbers.**

45 forty-five

1 33 thirty-three

2 98 ninety-eight

3 72 seventy-two

4 21 twenty-one

5 60 sixty

## Ordinal numbers

**9** ★★ **Write the ordinal numbers.**

1st first

1 3rd third

2 7th seventh

3 9th ninth

4 11th eleventh

5 12th twelfth

## Days of the week

**10** ★★ **Put the days of the week in order.**

Friday 5

Sunday 7

Thursday 4

Wednesday 3

Monday 1

Saturday 6

Tuesday 2

**11** ★★★ **Write true answers.**

What days are the weekend?

Saturday, Sunday

1 What days are your English classes?

Students' answers

2 What days are your maths classes?

3 What's your favourite school day?

## Months and seasons

**12** ★★ **Complete the words. Then match the seasons and the months.**

October

1 January

2 April

3 August

a) winter

b) autumn

c) summer

d) spring

## Countries and nationalities

**13** ★ **Are the words countries or nationalities? Write C or N.**

Greek N

1 French N

2 China C

3 Canada C

4 Italian N

5 the USA C

**14** ★★ **Match the parts of the words.**

Americ

1 Ja

2 Chin

3 Canad

4 Sp

5 Gre

a) ain

b) ese

c) an

d) pan

e) ece

f) ian

## Telling the time

**15** ★★★ **Write the times.**

06:15

It's quarter past six.

09:00

1 It's nine o'clock.

12:30

2 It's half past twelve.

05:45

3 It's quarter to six.

11:20

4 It's twenty past eleven.

09:50

5 It's ten to ten.

## *be*: present simple

**1** ★ **Choose the correct options.**

It **aren't** / **(isn't)** Saturday today.

1 Tom and I **'m** / **(are)** best friends.
2 I **isn't** / **('m not)** Portuguese.
3 My parents **isn't** / **(aren't)** good at English.
4 You **('re)** / **'s** from France.

**2** ★ **Match the questions and the answers.**

Is he your friend? b)

1 Are your books open? c)
2 Is it your pen? a)
3 Are you Japanese? d)

a) Yes, it is.
b) No, he isn't.
c) Yes, they are.
d) No, I'm not.

**3** ★★ **Write sentences. Use the correct forms of *be*.**

He / not / a student. He / a teacher.
He isn't a student. He's a teacher.

1 They / not / dogs. They / cats.
They aren't dogs. They're cats.

2 I / not / at school. I / in my house.
I'm not at school. I'm in my house.

3 We / not / American. We / Canadian.
We aren't American. We're Canadian.

4 It / not / my book. It / your book.
It isn't my book. It's your book.

5 You / not fourteen years old. You / twelve years old.
You aren't fourteen years old. You're twelve years old.

**4** ★★ **Complete the questions. Use the correct forms of *be*. Then write short answers.**

| Mark and Deb | Cody |
|---|---|
| 13 | 22 |
| British | American |
| students | actor |

Are Mark and Deb 13?
Yes, they are.

1 Is Cody 23?
No, he isn't.

2 Are Mark and Deb from the UK?
Yes, they are.

3 Is Cody from Canada?
No, he isn't.

4 Are Mark and Deb teachers?
No, they aren't.

5 Is Cody an actor?
Yes, he is.

**5** ★★★ **Complete the questions. Use the correct forms of *be*. Then write true answers.**

Are you in the classroom?
Yes, I am.
**or**
No, I'm not. I'm in my house.

1 Is it Sunday today?
Students' answers

2 Are you at home?

3 Are your parents at home?

4 Are you in an English exam?

5 Is your teacher Spanish?


**Grammar Bank** pages 63–65

## Possessive 's

**6** ★ **Write phrases. Use the possessive 's.**

| | |
|---|---|
| the girl | classroom |
| 1 the girls | apple |
| 2 the teacher | pencils |
| 3 the boy | bags |
| 4 the boys | pens |

the girl's pencils

1 the girls' pens

2 the teacher's bags

3 the boy's apple

4 the boys' classroom

**7** ★★ **Complete the sentences. Use 's or s'.**

The **boy**'s rubber is in his pencil case.

1 My **parent**s' names are Pat and Harry.

2 **Paul**'s notebook is red.

3 The **girl**'s name is Juliet.

4 My **sister**s' names are Alice and Jenny.

5 My **friend**s' CD players are in their bags.

**8** ★★★ **Write sentences. Add 's or ' in the correct places.**

The dog name / Blackie.
The dog's name is Blackie.

1 These / not / the students books.
These aren't the students' books.

2 My teacher eyes / brown.
My teacher's eyes are brown.

3 The girls bags / black.
The girls' bags are black.

4 I / not Tom sister.
I'm not Tom's sister.

5 My best friend name / Rafa.
My best friend's name is Rafa.

6 These / my teachers bags.
These are my teachers' bags.

## Demonstrative pronouns

**9** ★ **Look at the picture. Choose the correct options.**

(This) / That is my rubber.

1 These / (Those) are my dogs.

2 (This) / These is my desk.

3 (These) / Those are my pencils.

4 This / (That) is my CD player.

**10** ★★ **Look at the picture. Complete the sentences. Use *this*, *that*, *these* and *those*.**

This is my chair.

1 Those are my comics.

2 That is my friend, Anne.

3 This is my pencil case.

4 These are my pens.

**11** ★★★ **Look at the picture. Write sentences. Use *this*, *that*, *these* and *those*.**

(ruler) This is Cathy's ruler.

1 (umbrella) That is Cathy's umbrella.

2 (books) Those are Cathy's books.

3 (cats) These are Cathy's cats.

4 (notebook) This is Cathy's notebook.

## Meeting people

**1** ★ **Complete the dialogue. Use the phrases in the box.**

~~My name's Josh~~ Nice to meet you too
Oh, really Welcome to our school
Where are you from

| | |
|---|---|
| **Josh** | Hi! *My name's Josh.* |
| **Hannah** | Hello, Josh. My name's Hannah. |
| **Josh** | Nice to meet you. |
| **Hannah** | (**1**) Nice to meet you too. Are you from Oxford? |
| **Josh** | Yes, I am. And you? (**2**) Where are you from? |
| **Hannah** | I'm from Canada. |
| **Josh** | (**3**) Oh, really? Are you Canadian? |
| **Hannah** | Yes, I am. |
| **Josh** | (**4**) Welcome to our school! |
| **Hannah** | Thanks! |

**2** ★★ **Complete the sentences.**

The boy's name is *Josh.*

1 The girl's name is Hannah.
2 The boy is from Oxford.
3 The girl is from Canada. She is Canadian.

**3** ★★★ **In your notebook, write a dialogue like the dialogue in exercise 1. Use the ideas in the box.**

| Name | From |
|---|---|
| Chloe | Cambridge, the UK |
| Louis | France |

**4** ★ **Match the questions and the answers.**

Who is your favourite actor? *d)*

1 What is your favourite colour? g)
2 When is your birthday? a)
3 What are your favourite animals? b)
4 Where are you from? f)
5 Who is your favourite singer? e)
6 What's your name? c)

**a)** 21 August
**b)** dogs
**c)** Sara
**d)** Will Smith
**e)** Beyoncé
**f)** Greece
**g)** pink

**5** ★★ **Put the words in order.**

name? / your / What's
*What's your name?*

1 you / Where / from? / are
Where are you from?
2 birthday? / your / is / When
When is your birthday?
3 actor? / favourite / your / is / Who
Who is your favourite actor?
4 your / is / Who / singer? / favourite
Who is your favourite singer?
5 your / is / What / colour? / favourite
What is your favourite colour?
6 favourite / your / are / What / animals?
What are your favourite animals?

**6** ★★★ **Write true answers to the questions in exercise 5.**

What's your name?
*Blanca.*

1 Students' answers
2 
3 
4 
5 
6 

# 1 Look at me!

## Vocabulary

### Faces

**1** ★ **Complete the sentences. Use the picture.**

*Sam* has got dark hair.

1 Debra ______ has got a long nose.
2 Sam ______ has got big eyes.
3 Debra ______ has got short, dark hair.
4 Debra ______ has got freckles.
5 Sam ______ and Evan ______ have got glasses.
6 Evan ______ has got short, fair hair.
7 Sam ______ has got long hair.

**2** ★★ **Put the letters in order to complete the sentences. Use the picture.**

Mark has got big *eyes* (esey).

1 Mark and Nelly have got white teeth ______ (eetth).
2 Mark has got glasses ______ (sasslge).
3 Mark has got short, dark ______ (kdra) hair ______ (iahr).
4 Nelly has got long ______ (lngo), fair ______ (iraf) hair.
5 Nelly has got freckles ______ (rselfkec) on her nose ______ (eson).

**3** ★★★ **Complete true sentences about you and people you know.**

I've got *long, brown* hair.

1 My Students' answers are white.
2 ______ has got dark ______ .
3 My dad's got ______ , ______ hair.
4 ______ has got brown ______ and fair hair.
5 ______ has got ______ .
6 ______ has got ______ on his / her nose.

Vocabulary Bank pages 84–85

## have got

**1** ★ **Choose the correct options.**

I **('ve)** / **'s** got a small nose.

1 You **('ve)** / **'s** got new glasses.
2 Your sister **'ve** / **('s)** got freckles.
3 Our school **have** / **(has)** got 21 classrooms.
4 Alex and I **(have)** / **has** got new T-shirts.
5 My brothers **(have)** / **has** got MP3 players.

**2** ★ **Put the words in the correct order.**

1 a photo of our family / got / we / have / ?
Have we got a photo of our family?
2 have / I / a rubber in my pencil case / got / ?
Have I got a rubber in my pencil case?
3 got / have / a best friend / you / ?
Have you got a best friend?
4 has / short hair / got / your teacher / ?
Has your teacher got short hair?
5 your school / has / a computer room / got / ?
Has your school got a computer room?
6 long hair / have / got / your sisters / ?
Have your sisters got long hair?

**3** ★ **Match the answers below and the questions in exercise 2.**

Yes, we have. 1

a) No, they haven't. It's short. 6
b) Yes, it has. It's very good. 5
c) No, I haven't. 2
d) Yes, she has. 4
e) Yes, you have. His name's David. 3

**4** ★★ **Make the sentences affirmative (✓) or negative (✗).**

I've got a favourite colour. ✗
I haven't got a favourite colour.

1 Simon hasn't got blue eyes. ✓
Simon's got blue eyes.
2 Elephants have got small ears. ✗
Elephants haven't got small ears.
3 You haven't got a white T-shirt. ✓
You've got a white T-shirt.
4 We've got a dog. ✗
We haven't got a dog.
5 Mrs Black has got red hair. ✗
Mrs Black hasn't got red hair.

**5** ★★ **Write questions and short answers. Use the correct forms of *have got*.**

| | Ben | Anna | Kim and Chris |
|---|---|---|---|
| cat | ✗ | ✓ | ✗ |
| computer | ✓ | ✗ | ✓ |

Ben / a cat
Has Ben got a cat?
No, he hasn't.

1 Anna / a computer
Has Anna got a computer?
No, she hasn't.
2 Ben / a computer
Has Ben got a computer?
Yes, he has.
3 Kim and Chris / a computer
Have Kim and Chris got a computer?
Yes, they have.
4 Anna / a cat
Has Anna got a cat?
Yes, she has.
5 Kim and Chris / cat
Have Kim and Chris got a cat?
No, they haven't.


Grammar Bank pages 66–67

**6** ★★★ **Complete the dialogues. Use the correct forms of *have got*.**

**Julie** *Have* you *got* Mrs Brown for French classes?

**Owen** No, we (**1**) haven't. We (**2**) 've got a new teacher.

**Julie** Who?

**Owen** His name's Mr Davies. He (**3**) 's got black glasses.

**Julie** I know him. (**4**) Has he got dark hair?

**Owen** No, he (**5**) hasn't. He (**6**) 's got short, fair hair. He's nice.

**Mel** (**7**) Have I got your mobile phone number?

**Glen** No, you (**8**) haven't. Here it is.

**Mel** (**9**) Have you got my number?

**Glen** Yes, I (**10**) have. Is this it?

**Mel** Yes, that's right. (**11**) Has your phone got a camera?

**Glen** Yes, it (**12**) has. Look.

**7** ★★★ **Write true answers.**

Has your teacher got long hair?

*Yes, she has. She's got long, dark hair.*

**or**

*No, she hasn't. She's got short, dark hair.*

1 Have you got a brother or a sister?

Students' answers

2 Have you got a computer?

3 Has your teacher got a bicycle?

4 Have your friends got pink bags?

5 Has your best friend got freckles?

# Pronouns and possessive adjectives

**8** ★ **Match the words.**

| | | |
|---|---|---|
| | I | his |
| 1 | you | my |
| 2 | he | our |
| 3 | she | its |
| 4 | it | their |
| 5 | we | her |
| 6 | they | your |

**9** ★★ **Choose the correct options.**

This is **we** / **our** school.

1 **It** / **Its** name is The City School.

2 **She** / **Her** has got green eyes.

3 Have **they** / **their** got dark hair?

4 This is **you** / **your** notebook.

5 **It's** / **Its** quarter to one.

6 **He** / **His** hair is red.

7 Are **you** / **your** her sister?

8 What are **they** / **their** names?

9 **I** / **My** best friend has got freckles.

**10** ★★★ **Complete the sentences. Use pronouns and possessive adjectives.**

**Amy** Who's that boy?

**Joe** Where?

**Amy** He's got glasses. (**1**) They 're black.

**Joe** Oh! (**2**) His name's Paul. (**3**) He 's new.

**Amy** Is he in (**4**) your class?

**Joe** No, he isn't. He's in (**5**) my sister's class.

**Amy** Your sister's class? But (**6**) she 's in Year 7. So he's eleven years old!

**Joe** Yes. (**7**) He 's very big!

## Family

**1** ★ **Study the family tree. Then choose the correct options.**

Alec is Laura's **cousin** / **(uncle)**.

1 Rachel is George's **son** / **(daughter)**.
2 Kate is Nick's **husband** / **(wife)**.
3 Mary is Josh's **(grandmother)** / **grandfather**.
4 Rachel is Josh's **(aunt)** / **uncle**.
5 Harry and Mary are Ellie's **(grandparents)** / **parents**.
6 Josh is Hector's **brother** / **(cousin)**.
7 Rachel is Iris's **(mum)** / **dad**.

**2** ★★ **Study the family tree in exercise 1. Then complete the sentences.**

Anna is Iris's grandma.

1 Laura's got three u n c l e s .
2 Josh's a u n t is Rachel.
3 Simon's w i f e is Rachel.
4 Rachel and Simon have got one s o n .
5 Rachel's p a r e n t s are George and Anna.
6 Iris is Simon's d a u g h t e r .
7 Hector is Laura's b r o t h e r .
8 Alec and Paul have got one s i s t e r .
9 George is Paul's d a d .
10 Josh and Ellie have got three c o u s i n s .

**3** ★★★ **Answer the questions to write definitions.**

Who is your mum's husband?
My mum's husband is my dad.

1 Who is your mum's father?
My mum's father is my grandfather / grandpa.

2 Who is your dad's mother?
My dad's mother is my grandmother / grandma.

3 Who are your parents' brothers and sisters?
My parents' brothers and sisters are my aunts and uncles.

4 Who are your aunt's sons and daughters?
My aunt's sons and daughters are my cousins.

5 Who is your uncle's wife?
My uncle's wife is my aunt.

6 Who are your father's mother and father?
My father's mother and father are my grandparents.

 Vocabulary Bank pages 84–85

# Three families

**1 How big is your family?**

| | |
|---|---|
| Gisella | We've got a small family: Mum, Dad and me. I haven't got a brother or sister. I've got a cat. He's sixteen years old – the same as me. |
| Alan | There are six people in my family – me, my parents, my brother, and my two little sisters. My mum, my dad, my brother and I have got dark hair. My sisters have got fair hair. |
| Oliver | We've got a big family! I've got three brothers, James, Callum and Andrew. James and Callum are twins. I've also got two sisters. I've got glasses, like my mum and dad. |

a)

b)

c)

**2 ★ Read the text. Match the families in the photos and the names.**

Gisella *b)*

1 Alan c)

2 Oliver a)

**3 ★★ Are these sentences true or false? Write T or F.**

Gisella has got a brother. *F*

1 Gisella's cat is male. T

2 Gisella is fourteen years old. F

3 Alan's sisters have got dark hair. F

4 There are eight people in Oliver's family. T

5 James and Callum are the same age. T

6 Oliver hasn't got glasses. F

**4 ★★★ Answer the questions.**

How many people are there in Gisella's family?

*There are three people and a cat.*

1 How old is Gisella?

Gisella is sixteen years old.

2 Has she got a sister?

No, she hasn't.

3 How many brothers has Alan got?

He's got one brother.

4 Has Alan got fair hair?

No, he hasn't. He's got dark hair.

5 How many people have got glasses in Oliver's family?

Three people have got glasses.

6 Who are the twins in Oliver's family?

James and Callum are the twins.

## Asking to borrow things

**1** ★ **Complete the dialogue. Use the sentences in the box.**

Can I borrow it, please
~~Have you got a rubber~~ No, I haven't
Yes, I have You're welcome

| | |
|---|---|
| **Gav** | Jess! *Have you got a rubber?* |
| **Jess** | (1) No, I haven't. Sorry! Ask Lucy. |
| **Gav** | OK. ... Lucy! |
| **Lucy** | Yes? |
| **Gav** | Have you got a rubber? |
| **Lucy** | (2) Yes, I have. |
| **Gav** | (3) Can I borrow it, please? |
| **Lucy** | Of course. Here you are. |
| **Gav** | Thank you! |
| **Lucy** | (4) You're welcome! |

**2** ★★ **Answer the questions.**

Has Gav got a rubber?
*No, he hasn't.*

1 Has Jess got a rubber?
No, she hasn't.

2 Has Lucy got a rubber?
Yes, she has.

**3** ★★★ **In your notebook, write a dialogue like the dialogue in exercise 1. Use one of the ideas in the pictures.**

## Dictation

**4** ★★ 4.02 **Listen. Listen again and write the sentences in your notebook.**



## Order of adjectives

**1** ★ **Correct the mistakes.**

black, big cat *big, black cat*

1 white, big rubber big, white rubber
2 blue, big eyes big, blue eyes
3 dark, short hair short, dark hair
4 fair, long hair long, fair hair

**2** ★★ **Put the words in the correct order.**

bag. / big, / She's / pink / got a
*She's got a big, pink bag.*

1 blue / Have you / small, / got / pen? / my
Have you got my small, blue pen?

2 your / got / notebook. / red / I've / big,
I've got your big, red notebook.

3 got / little, / mobile phone. / He's / a / black
He's got a little, black mobile phone.

4 your / pencil? / green / Can I borrow / short,
Can I borrow your short, green pencil?

**3** ★★★ **Study the photo. Then complete the email.**

Hi Andy,

This is my family. I've got **dark** eyes and (1) long, dark hair – and my big sister, Sharon, has got (2) dark eyes and (3) long, dark hair too! My mum's name is Suzie. She's got (4) short, dark hair and she's got (5) glasses. My (6) grandmother's / grandma's name is Michelle. She's got (7) short, grey hair.

Write to me!

Jenny

 Writing Builder page 102

# 2 At the weekend

## Vocabulary

### Free time

**1** ★ **Complete the words. Use the pictures.**

watch TV

1 d o puzz l e s

2 pl a y the pi a n o

3 g o sk a t e b o a r d ing

4 ch a t on the In t e r n e t

5 m e e t fr i e n d s

**2** ★★ **Complete the crossword.**

| | | | | | | | | | |
|---|---|---|---|---|---|---|---|---|---|
| | | 1 P | | 2 M | | | | | |
| | 3 C | I | N | E | M | A | | | |
| | | A | | E | | | | | |
| | | N | | T | | | | 4 I | |
| | 5 G | O | | | 6 P | H | O | N | E |
| | A | | | | U | | | T | |
| | 7 M | A | G | A | Z | I | N | E | S |
| | E | | | | Z | | | R | |
| | S | | | | L | | | N | |
| | | | | | E | | | E | |
| 8 M | O | D | E | L | S | | | T | |

1 play the *piano*
2 meet friends
3 go to the cinema
4 chat on the Internet
5 → go skateboarding
5 ↓ play computer games
6 → talk on the phone
6 ↓ do puzzles
7 read magazines
8 make models

**3** ★★★ **Complete the sentences.**

I *watch TV*. My favourite comedy is *The Simpsons*.

1 I go to the cinema. I love comedy films.
2 I listen to music. I've got an MP3 player with 10,000 songs!
3 I chat on the Internet. I've got a good computer and I meet new people from different countries.
4 I do puzzles. Crosswords are my favourite.

## Present simple affirmative

**1** ★ **Choose the correct options.**

You and your brother **(watch)** / **watches** TV a lot.

1 Harry and I **(go)** / **goes** to the same school.
2 My uncle **speak** / **(speaks)** three languages.
3 I **(live)** / **lives** in Granada.
4 My sister **study** / **(studies)** French and Spanish at university.
5 You **(use)** / **uses** the Internet a lot.
6 They **(teach)** / **teaches** Greek at my school.

**2** ★ **Complete the chart. Use the third person singular of the verbs in the box.**

carry do ~~make~~ play speak study teach watch

| + *s* | + *es* | *y* → *ies* |
|---|---|---|
| makes | (3) does | (6) carries |
| (1) plays | (4) teaches | (7) studies |
| (2) speaks | (5) watches | |

**3** ★★ **Complete the sentences. Use the correct forms of the verbs in brackets.**

Jack's dad makes good models. (make)

1 The TV programme finishes at half past six. (finish)
2 I study a lot for my exams. (study)
3 My mum chats to my grandma on the Internet. (chat)
4 We do puzzles in the evening. (do)
5 Kaka plays football for Real Madrid. (play)
6 My aunt teaches English. (teach)
7 You and your brother speak good English. (speak)
8 My teacher carries our books. (carry)

**4** ★★ **Complete the text. Use the correct forms of the verbs in the box.**

carry like listen ~~love~~ play prefer sing teach think

My sister loves music. She **(1)** carries her MP3 player all the time. She **(2)** listens to a lot of music from different countries. I **(3)** prefer music in English but she also **(4)** likes Spanish and Italian pop music. We both **(5)** think Laura Pausini is good.

We're in a music group with some friends. My sister **(6)** plays the guitar and I **(7)** sing. I can't play the guitar but my sister **(8)** teaches me on Saturdays. She's very good.

**5** ★★★ **Complete true sentences. Use the verbs in the box.**

carry chat finish ~~live~~ make study watch

I live in Spain.

1 My parents Students' answers ________.
2 On Saturday, classes ________.
3 My teacher ________.
4 My best friend ________.
5 The students in my class ________.
6 My best friend and I ________.


Grammar Bank pages 68–69

## Adverbs of frequency

**6** ★ **Cross out the extra words.**

I never do ~~never~~ my homework on Saturday evenings.

1 Olivia ~~sometimes~~ is sometimes in the park on Sundays.

2 The TV programme always finishes ~~always~~ at six o'clock.

3 I ~~usually~~ am usually at home on Sunday evenings.

4 That boy ~~almost never~~ is almost never at school.

**7** ★★ **Rewrite the sentences. Use the words in the box.**

| almost never | always | ~~never~~ | often | sometimes | usually |
|---|---|---|---|---|---|

She finishes her homework. ○○○○○
She never finishes her homework.

1 I do puzzles. ●●○○○
I sometimes do puzzles.

2 We're in the park on Sundays. ●●●○○
We're often in the park on Sundays.

3 I'm at home on Saturday evenings. ●○○○○
I'm almost never at home on Saturday evenings.

4 I carry my MP3 player. ●●●●●
I always carry my MP3 player.

5 He invites me to his parties. ●●●●○
He usually invites me to his parties.

**8** ★★★ **Write true sentences. Use a different adverb of frequency in each sentence.**

I love the cinema. I always go to the cinema on Saturdays.

1 I think Students' answers is OK. I __________
__________.

2 My dad hates __________. He __________
__________.

3 My mum hates __________. She __________
__________.

## *can / can't*

**9** ★ **Put the words in the correct order.**

speak / you / Spanish? / Can
Can you speak Spanish?

1 can / Josh / good models. / make
Josh can make good models.

2 we / Can / the computer? / use
Can we use the computer?

3 this exercise. / do / can't / I
I can't do this exercise.

4 meet / can't / Rob / you today.
Rob can't meet you today.

**10** ★★ **Make the sentences affirmative (✓), negative (✗) or interrogative (?).**

I can't carry this bag. ✓
I can carry this bag.

1 I can meet friends at twelve o'clock. ?
Can I meet friends at twelve o'clock?

2 Can Martin and Paul sing? ✓
Martin and Paul can sing.

3 You can do this puzzle. ?
Can you do this puzzle?

4 My grandparents can speak English. ✗
My grandparents can't speak English.

5 I can't play the guitar. ✓
I can play the guitar.

6 Can Jenny play basketball? ✗
Jenny can't play basketball.

**11** ★★★ **Read the sentences. Write what you say next. Use *can* or *can't* and your own ideas.**

'This exercise is difficult. I can't understand it.' ✗

1 'Your English is good! Students' answers __________
__________.' ✓

2 'My friends are in the park. __________
__________?'

3 'You never finish your homework. __________
__________.' ✗

4 'I can speak Spanish and English. __________
__________?'

## Sports

**1 ★ Choose the correct options.**

(water polo) / swimming

1 athletics / (gymnastics)

2 skiing / (ice skating)

3 (aerobics) / martial arts

4 (hockey) / tennis

5 basketball / (volleyball)

**2 ★★ Complete the sentences. Use the words in the box.**

athletics football ~~go cycling~~ go skiing martial arts tennis

I've got a bicycle. I *go cycling* every day.

1 Athletics is my favourite sport. I can run 100 metres in fourteen seconds.

2 Our favourite sport is tennis. Our favourite player is Rafael Nadal.

3 I watch football on Saturdays. My favourite team is Chelsea.

4 My brother loves martial arts. He does judo.

5 We go skiing in the winter in Pradollano, near Granada.

**3 ★★★ Write sentences about the people in the pictures.**

Karen *does martial arts.*

1 Macy and Lauren play basketball.

2 Sally goes swimming.

3 Jack and Ruby go skiing.



Vocabulary Bank pages 86–87

# At the weekend

**1 What is your favourite time at the weekend?**

Paula Lopez is a famous Argentinean skateboarder. What does she do at weekends?

'I'm never bored at weekends. I go to school on Saturday morning. Classes finish at eleven o'clock. I meet my friends Lucas and Carlos at the park. We go skateboarding. Then in the afternoon we go to the cinema. We watch a comedy film. In the evening, I write emails to my fans.

On Sunday morning, I go skateboarding again! I've got a small skateboarding park in my garden. I practice and I listen to music on my MP3 player. In the afternoon, I study English. My dad helps me. In the evening, I play the guitar with my brother. He's good at the guitar. I'm not!

**2 ★ Read the text. Tick (✓) the activities that are in the text.**

meet friends ✓

1 play computer games
2 chat on the Internet
3 go the cinema ✓
4 listen to music ✓
5 watch TV
6 play the guitar ✓

**3 ★★ Put the events in Paula's weekend in the correct order.**

1 Paula plays the guitar. 7
2 Paula goes skateboarding in her garden. 5
3 Paula writes emails. 4
4 Paula goes to school. 1
5 Paula studies English. 6
6 Paula watches a film. 3
7 Paula goes to the park. 2

**4 ★★ Are these sentences true or false? Write T or F.**

Paula's classes finish at one o'clock. F

1 Lucas can skateboard. T
2 Paula has got an MP3 player. T
3 Paula's father can speak English. T
4 Paula's brother can't play the guitar. F

**5 ★★★ Complete the summary of Paula's weekend.**

On Saturday morning, Paula goes to school.

1 After school, she meets friends and goes skateboarding.
2 On Saturday afternoon, she goes to the cinema.
3 On Saturday evening, she writes emails to her fans.
4 On Sunday morning, she goes skateboarding.
5 On Sunday afternoon, she studies English.
6 On Sunday evening, she plays the guitar with her brother.

## Making arrangements

**1** ★ **Put the sentences in the correct order.**

| | |
|---|---|
| **Alex** | Great! See you there! Bye! 7 |
| **Alex** | Let's go to the sports centre. We can play water polo. 3 |
| **Alex** | It's half past eleven. 5 |
| **Alex** | I'm bored! 1 |
| **Olivia** | Me too! What can we do this afternoon? 2 |
| **Olivia** | Bye! 8 |
| **Olivia** | Good idea! What time is it now? 4 |
| **Olivia** | OK. Let's meet at the sports centre at twelve o'clock. 6 |

**2** ★★ **Are these sentences true or false? Write T or F.**

Alex and Olivia are bored. T

1 Alex wants to go swimming. F

2 Olivia thinks Alex's idea is good. T

3 It's 11:30 a.m. now. T

4 Olivia wants to meet at the sports centre. T

5 Olivia wants to meet in an hour. F

**3** ★★★ **In your notebook, write a dialogue like the dialogue in exercise 1. Use the ideas in the box.**

**suggestion:** go windsurfing **place:** at the beach
**time now:** 9 a.m. **time to meet:** 10:30 a.m.

## Dictation

**4** ★★ 4.03 **Listen. Listen again and write the sentences in your notebook.**



## Prepositions of time

**1** ★ **Choose the correct options.**

I play football (at) / **on** three o'clock.

1 We're always happy **in** / (**on**) Friday.

2 I usually meet my friends **in** / (**at**) the weekend.

3 I always do my homework (**on**) / **at** Sunday evening.

4 We almost never watch TV (**in**) / **on** the morning.

**2** ★★ **Complete the sentences. Use *at*, *in* and *on*.**

The film starts at eight o'clock.

1 My sister does martial arts on Sundays.

2 My parents do puzzles in the evening.

3 We play water polo on Sunday afternoons.

4 I'm always happy at the weekend.

5 We often go ice skating in the afternoon.

**3** ★★★ **Study the diary. Then complete the description of a weekend. Use prepositions and time phrases.**

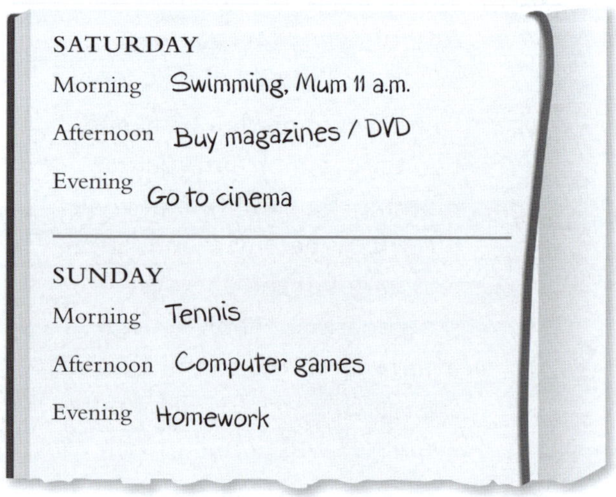


On Saturday morning, my dad and I go swimming. (**1**) At eleven o'clock, we meet my mum at the shopping centre. (**2**) In the afternoon, I buy some magazines or a DVD. (**3**) In the evening, we go to the cinema. (**4**) On Sunday morning, my big brother and I play tennis. (**5**) In the afternoon, I play computer games. (**6**) In the evening, I often do my homework.


Writing Builder page 103

# 3 Time for school

## Vocabulary

### Weekday routine

**1 ★ Match the words and the pictures.**

do homework get dressed ~~get up~~
go to bed have a shower have breakfast
leave home start classes

*get up*

1 have a shower

2 get dressed

3 have breakfast

4 leave home

5 start classes

6 do homework

7 go to bed

**2 ★★ Complete the text. Use the words in the boxes.**

~~get up~~ have a shower start classes
leave home have breakfast

I *get up* at half past seven in the morning. I always (**1**) have a shower before I get dressed. Then I (**2**) have breakfast – I like a lot of food!

I always cycle to school and I (**3**) leave home at half past eight. We (**4**) start classes at nine o'clock. On Monday my first class is French.

do my homework finish classes
go home go to bed have a break
have dinner have lunch

At quarter to eleven we (**5**) have a break. I usually talk to friends about my weekend. At half past twelve we (**6**) have lunch in the school canteen.

At half past three we (**7**) finish classes and I (**8**) go home. At home I usually watch TV and then I (**9**) do my homework. At seven o'clock my dad comes home and I (**10**) have dinner with my family. We talk about our days. Then at half past ten I (**11**) go to bed.

**3 ★★★ Write true sentences about your weekday routine.**

*I get up at half past seven.*

1 Students' answers
2 ______
3 ______
4 ______
5 ______

# Present simple negative and interrogative

**1** ★ **Choose the correct options.**

My grandpa **don't** / **(doesn't)** use email.

1 My sister doesn't **(like)** / **likes** magazines.
2 My aunt and uncle **(don't)** / **doesn't** have a TV.
3 Our school **don't** / **(doesn't)** have Spanish classes.
4 We **(don't)** / **doesn't** have classes on Saturday and Sunday.
5 Adam doesn't **(have)** / **has** breakfast on Sunday mornings.

**2** ★ **Match the questions and the answers. Use the chart.**

| On weekdays | Jack | Grace | Lily and Tom |
|---|---|---|---|
| have breakfast with family | ✓ | ✗ | ✓ |
| take a bus to school | ✗ | ✓ | ✗ |
| do homework before dinner | ✗ | ✓ | ✓ |
| read in bed | ✓ | ✗ | ✗ |

Does Jack have breakfast with his family? d)

1 Do Lily and Tom take a bus to school? a)
2 Does Jack take a bus to school? f)
3 Does Grace do her homework before dinner? e)
4 Do Lily and Tom do their homework before dinner? b)
5 Does Grace read in bed? c)

a) No, they don't.
b) Yes, they do.
c) No, she doesn't.
d) Yes, he does.
e) Yes, she does.
f) No, he doesn't.

**3** ★★ **Write questions and short answers. Use the chart in exercise 2.**

Grace / breakfast with her family?
Does Grace have breakfast with her family?
No, she doesn't.

1 Lily and Tom / in bed?
Do Lily and Tom read in bed?
No, they don't.
2 Grace / a bus to school?
Does Grace take a bus to school?
Yes, she does.
3 Jack / his homework before dinner?
Does Jack do his homework before dinner?
No, he doesn't.
4 Lily and Tom / breakfast with their family?
Do Lily and Tom have breakfast with their family?
Yes, they do.
5 Jack / in bed?
Does Jack read in bed?
Yes, he does.

**4** ★★ **Write negative sentences. Use the words in brackets.**

Kirstie studies Spanish. (Italian)
She doesn't study Italian.

1 I know your sister. (brother)
I don't know your brother.
2 Macy and Olivia read magazines. (comics)
They don't read comics.
3 I do gymnastics. (athletics)
I don't do athletics.
4 Mrs García teaches English. (French)
She doesn't teach French.
5 We play football. (hockey)
We don't play hockey.
6 The class starts at ten o'clock. (half past ten)
It doesn't start at half past ten.
7 You sit next to Paul. (Rob)
You don't sit next to Rob.


Grammar Bank pages 70–71

5 ★★★ **Write questions and true answers. Use *do* and *does*.**

you / hockey?
*Do you play hockey?*
*No, I don't. Our school doesn't teach hockey.*

1 your English teacher / dinner with you?
Students' answers ______________________
______________________

2 you / break at ten o'clock on Wednesdays?
______________________
______________________

3 your mum / English at your school?
______________________
______________________

4 you and your friends / Chinese?
______________________
______________________

5 your parents / swimming classes?
______________________
______________________

6 Jasper and I / technology after history?
______________________
______________________

## Question words

6 ★ **Match the questions and the answers.**

Why do your parents study English? f)
1 What does Joe read? b)
2 How often do you read books? a)
3 Who does Martin sit next to in English class? e)
4 When does your English class start? d)
5 Where do you read? c)

a) Every day.
b) Books and magazines.
c) In my bedroom.
d) At nine o'clock.
e) Simon.
f) Because they like England.

7 ★★ **Complete the questions. Use the words in the box.**

| How often | What | When | ~~Where~~ | Who | Why |
|---|---|---|---|---|---|

*Where* do you live?
In Oxford.

1 Who ________ do you meet on Saturdays?
Our friend, Luis.

2 What ________ does Brandon do after he gets up?
He has a shower.

3 Why ________ does Bélèn chat to her grandpa on the Internet?
Because he lives in England.

4 When ________ does Ruby get dressed on weekdays?
At eight o'clock.

5 How often ________ do you take a bus to school?
Almost never.

8 ★★★ **Write questions for the answers.**

*Where does he live?*
He lives in Seville.

1 Why does John like maths?
John likes maths because it's interesting.

2 Who do you sit with?
I sit with my best friend, Macy.

3 Who do you usually have dinner with?
I usually have dinner with my parents.

4 What do you do after school?
After school I do my homework.

5 When does your school finish?
My school finishes at half past three.

## School subjects

**1** ★ **Complete the words. Use the picture.**

English

1 g e o g r a _p_ _h_ _y_
2 F r e n _c_ _h_
3 m u s _i_ _c_
4 s c i e n _c_ _e_
5 t e c h n o l _o_ _g_ _y_
6 I C _T_
7 h i s t _o_ _r_ _y_
8 m a t h _s_

**2** ★★ **Complete the puzzle. Use the pictures.**

| | | | | | | | | | | | |
|---|---|---|---|---|---|---|---|---|---|---|---|
| | | | | A | R | T | | | | | |
| | | | 1 | P | E | | | | | | |
| 2 | | M | U | S | I | C | | | | | |
| 3 | F | R | E | N | C | H | | | | | |
| 4 | | S | C | I | E | N | C | E | | | |
| 5 | | H | I | S | T | O | R | Y | | | |
| 6 | | | E | N | G | L | I | S | H | | |
| | | | | | | O | | | | | |
| 7 | | | G | E | O | G | R | A | P | H | Y |
| | | | | | | Y | | | | | |

4
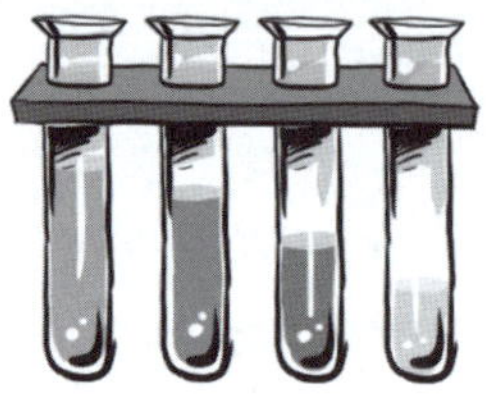

1

5

2

6

3

7

**3** ★★★ **Write sentences about school subjects. Use the words in the box.**

| |
|---|
| ~~animals and plants~~ computers Picasso the Romans trigonometry |

In science we study animals and plants.

1 _In ICT we study computers._
2 _In art we study Picasso._
3 _In history we study the Romans._
4 _In maths we study trigonometry._



Vocabulary Bank pages 88–89

# Our timetable

**1 What's your favourite weekday? Why?**

| | Monday | Tuesday | Wednesday | Thursday | Friday |
|---|---|---|---|---|---|
| 9:00 | science | PE | science | maths | science |
| 9:50 | maths | PE | science | science | English |
| 10:40 | break | | | | |
| 11:00 | French | English | maths | technology | ICT |
| 11:50 | geography | French | history | technology | maths |
| 12:40 | lunch | | | | |
| 1:40 | English | maths | art | music | geography |
| 2:30 | German | history | art | ICT | German |

*Nick*

*My favourite day is … . I've got French in the morning and German in the afternoon. They're my favourite subjects.*

*I love (1) … mornings. Computers are fun. But I don't enjoy the afternoons. We've got geography. I think it's difficult and the homework is boring. I always do it on Sunday evenings.*

**Lola**

(2) … is my favourite day because we do gymnastics or athletics in the morning. Then after lunch we've got maths. Maths is easy!

I hate (3) … . We've got science in the morning. Experiments are OK but Mr Clark always gives us difficult homework. Then before lunch it's history. Boring!

**2 ★ Read the text. Complete the text with the days in the box.**

Friday ~~Monday~~ Tuesday Wednesday

Monday
1 Friday
2 Tuesday
3 Wednesday

**3 ★★ Are these sentences true or false? Write T or F.**

Nick likes French but he doesn't like German. F

1 Nick likes ICT. T
2 Nick doesn't like geography. T
3 Nick enjoys geography homework. F
4 Lola likes sport. T
5 Lola is good at maths. T
6 Lola hates science experiments. F
7 Lola thinks history is boring. T

**4 ★★★ Answer the questions.**

When do Nick and Lola have art?
They have art on Wednesday afternoons.

1 Why does Nick love Friday mornings?
Because he's got ICT and he thinks computers are fun.

2 When does he do his geography homework?
On Sunday evenings.

3 What sports does Lola often do in PE?
She often does gymnastics or athletics.

4 Why does Lola like maths?
Because she thinks maths is easy.

5 What does Lola's science teacher always do?
He always gives them difficult homework.

## Giving opinions

**1** ★ **Put the sentences in the correct order.**

| | |
|---|---|
| **Grace** | What subjects do you like? 1 |
| **Grace** | Really? I don't like French. I think it's difficult. And I hate history because it's really boring. 3 |
| **Charlie** | I like technology, but I don't like maths. I'm not very good at it. 6 |
| **Grace** | I love technology. It's easy and it's fun. It's my favourite subject. I also like maths. 5 |
| **Charlie** | I like French. I think it's fun. And I love history. It's really interesting. 2 |
| **Charlie** | What subjects do you like? 4 |

**2** ★★ **Answer the questions.**

What subjects does Charlie like?
He likes French and he loves history.

1 Why does he like history?
He thinks it's really interesting.

2 Does Grace like history? Why?
No, she doesn't, because she thinks it's really boring.

3 What is Grace's favourite subject? Why?
Technology is Grace's favourite subject because she thinks it's easy and it's fun.

4 What subject do Charlie and Grace both like?
They both like technology.

5 Does Charlie like maths? Why?
No, he doesn't, because he's not very good at it.

**3** ★★★ **In your notebook, write a dialogue like the dialogue in exercise 1. Use subjects you like and subjects you don't like.**

## Dictation

**4** ★★ 4.04 **Listen. Listen again and write the sentences in your notebook.**

## Capital letters

**1** ★ **Choose the correct options.**

1 Our **technology** / **Technology** teacher is Mrs **white** / **White**.

2 My brother and **i** / **I** take a bus to school on **fridays** / **Fridays**.

3 **does** / **Does** your **mum** / **Mum** go cycling?

4 I don't study **german** / **German** but I study **science** / **Science**.

5 **my** / **My** birthday is in **february** / **February**.

6 My cousins are **french** / **French** and they live in **marseilles** / **Marseilles**.

**2** ★★ **Correct the mistakes. Use capital letters.**

my favourite day is tuesday because i've got pe.
My favourite day is Tuesday because I've got PE.

1 we often go to granada in spain in august.
We often go to Granada in Spain in August.

2 my mother is german but my father is english.
My mother is German but my father is English.

3 i meet my friend alex on saturday mornings.
I meet my friend Alex on Saturday mornings.

4 mr evans is my ict teacher.
Mr Evans is my ICT teacher.

**3** ★★★ **Correct the mistakes. Use capital letters.**

I go to Park School in ~~boston~~, ~~usa~~. I get up at seven o'clock. My first class on ~~monday~~ is Spanish. ~~american~~ students often learn French too. In ~~september~~ I start classes in ~~italian~~. Then we have science. We have lunch in the school canteen. In the afternoon ~~i~~ have ICT. The teacher is Mr ~~ball~~.

| | | | |
|---|---|---|---|
| | Boston | 4 | September |
| 1 | USA | 5 | Italian |
| 2 | Monday | 6 | I |
| 3 | American | 7 | Ball |



Writing Builder page 104

# 4 Put on your coat!

## Vocabulary

### Weather

**1** ★ **Complete the words. Use the pictures.**

cloudy

3 w _i_ n d _y_

1 _i_ c _y_

4 s n _o_ w _y_

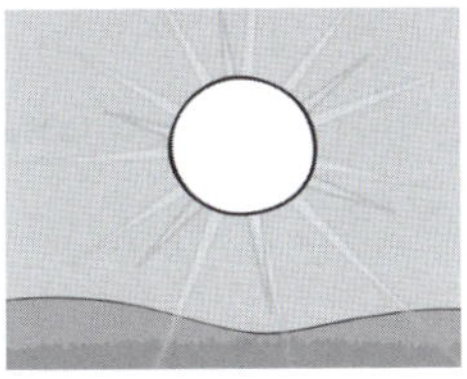
2 s _u_ n n _y_

5 r _a_ i n _y_

**2** ★★ **Complete the words. Use the pictures.**

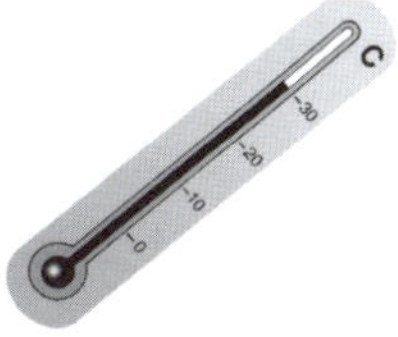
hot

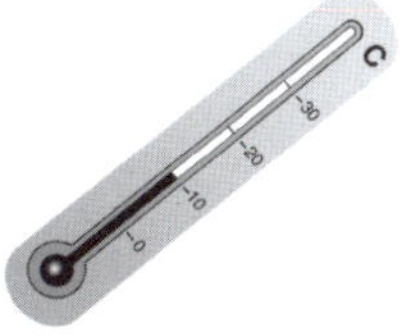
2 c _o_ _o_ _l_

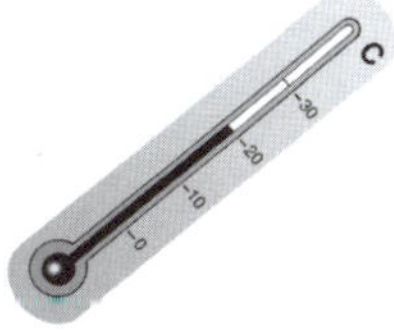
1 w _a_ _r_ _m_

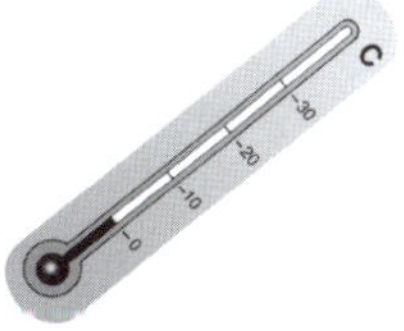
3 c _o_ _l_ _d_

**3** ★★ **Complete the crossword. Use the pictures.**

1 

5 

2 

6 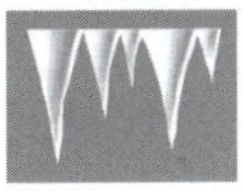

3 

7 

4 

**4** ★★★ **Write sentences about the places.**

World Forecast: 5th January

| Place | Temperature | Weather |
|---|---|---|
| Rio de Janeiro | 26°C |  |
| Montreal | –11°C |  |
| Los Angeles | 19°C |  |
| Athens | 12°C |  |

It's hot and sunny in Rio de Janeiro.

1 It's cold and snowy in Montreal.

2 It's warm and rainy in Los Angeles.

3 It's cool and cloudy in Athens.

# Present continuous

**1** ★ **Are these sentences affirmative, negative or interrogative? Write A, N or I.**

Am I sitting on your chair? I

1 Mark is getting up. A
2 My parents aren't going skiing. N
3 Is it raining? I
4 We're playing tennis at the park. A
5 The boys are doing their homework. A
6 My brother isn't going to classes. N
7 Are they wearing T-shirts? I
8 I'm not studying French. N

**2** ★ **Complete the chart. Use the *-ing* forms of the verbs in the box.**

~~dance~~ have make play put read sit stop study

| Normal | Final *e* | Short vowel + consonant |
|---|---|---|
| (1) playing | dancing | (6) putting |
| (2) reading | (4) having | (7) sitting |
| (3) studying | (5) making | (8) stopping |

**3** ★★ **Complete the sentences. Use the present continuous of the verbs in the box.**

chat go ~~listen~~ not live not watch not work rain sleep

You aren't listening to me.

1 They aren't watching TV at the moment.
2 It 's raining outside. Put on your coat.
3 The cat 's sleeping on my bed.
4 It's Saturday! Dad isn't working today.
5 We 're going to the cinema. Do you want to come?
6 My sister isn't living at our house at the moment. She's at university in London.
7 Mum is chatting to her friend on the phone.

**4** ★★ **Write questions and short answers. Use the present continuous.**

you / watch TV? ✓
Are you watching TV?
Yes, I am.

1 you and your brother / have / dinner? ✓
Are you and your brother having dinner?
Yes, we are.

2 Is / Robert / swim? ✗
Is Robert swimming?
No, he isn't.

3 those men / take / our car? ✗
Are those men taking our car?
No, they aren't.

4 Adam and Joe / do / their homework? ✓
Are Adam and Joe doing their homework?
Yes, they are.

5 your sister / wear / a green T-shirt? ✓
Is your sister wearing a green T-shirt?
Yes, she is.

**5** ★★★ **Write true answers about you and people you know.**

Are you listening to music at the moment?
No, I'm not. I'm doing my homework.

**or**

Are you wearing jeans at the moment?
Yes, I am. I'm wearing blue jeans.

1 Is your mum working at the moment?
Students' answers

2 Are you sitting on your bed at the moment?
__________

3 Is your teacher helping you at the moment?
__________

4 Is your dad using the Internet at the moment?
__________

5 Is your best friend walking to school at the moment?
__________

6 Is it snowing at the moment?
__________


Grammar Bank pages 72–73

## Present tense contrast

**6** ★ **Choose the correct options.**

Look! Martin **wears** / **'s wearing** your coat.

1 On Saturdays I **go** / **'m going** swimming.

2 '**Do they play** / **Are they playing** tennis?'
'No, they don't.'

3 'You **eat** / **'re eating** my sandwich.'
'Sorry. I'm very hungry.'

4 We **never buy** / **'re never buying** magazines.

**7** ★★ **Complete the sentences. Use the present simple or the present continuous.**

'Holà!'
'Sorry, I don't speak Spanish.' (I / not / speak / Spanish)

1 'Do you make models?' (you / make / models)
'No, never.'

2 'Goodnight! I'm going to bed.' (I / go / to bed)

3 'Sarah! Are you getting up?' (you / get up)

4 Every morning, Simon gets up at seven o'clock. (Simon / get up)

5 'I can't talk now. We're having dinner.' (we / have / dinner)

6 On Saturdays they don't have classes. (they / not / have / classes)

**8** ★★★ **Complete the sentences. Use the present simple or the present continuous affirmative.**

1 I usually get up at 7:30 a.m. but today is Saturday. I 'm getting up at ten o'clock!

2 Mum 's taking us to school in the car today. We usually take the bus.

3 Amy usually sits behind Tom in class. Today she 's sitting next to him.

4 I usually have a shower before I have breakfast. Today I 'm having breakfast before my shower.

5 We 're doing martial arts in PE today. We usually do gymnastics.

## Prepositions of place

**9** ★ **Choose the correct options. Use the picture.**

The pens and pencils are **on** / **in** the desk.

1 The books are **under** / **in** the bag.

2 The bag is **behind** / **next to** the chair.

3 The pencil case is **in front of** / **behind** the notebook.

4 The boy is **in front of** / **on** the window.

**10** ★★ **Complete the sentences. Use the picture in exercise 9 and the words in the box.**

| behind | ~~in~~ | in front of | next to | on | under |
|---|---|---|---|---|---|

The football is in the bin.

1 The desk is next to the bin.

2 The pens are in front of the cat.

3 The T-shirt is on the computer.

4 The cat is behind the computer.

5 The chair is under the desk.

**11** ★★★ **Write true sentences about people and things in your classroom. Use prepositions of place.**

I sit in front of Marta.

1 Students' answers

2 ______

3 ______

4 ______

## Clothes

**1** ★ **Find the words.**

jumperaincoatrainersandalskirtrousersockshoes

| | |
|---|---|
| jumper | 4 skirt |
| 1 raincoat | 5 trousers |
| 2 trainers | 6 socks |
| 3 sandals | 7 shoes |

**2** ★★ **Complete the words. Then match the words and the pictures.**

scarf a)

1 s k i r t h)
2 s h o e s c)
3 j u m p e r g)
4 c o a t d)
5 b o o t s e)
6 s h o r t s b)
7 j a c k e t f)

a) 

e) 

b) 

f) 

c) 

g) 

d) 

h) 

**3** ★★★ **Complete the text. Use the picture.**

Welcome to the Clothes Show! We've got three models today: Joshua, Yasmine and Caitlin.

In the spring collection, Joshua's wearing brown **trousers** and a white (**1**) shirt . He's also wearing white (**2**) trainers and black (**3**) socks .

In the summer collection, Yasmine's wearing a beautiful summer (**4**) dress and, on her feet, red (**5**) sandals . She's also got a light (**6**) jacket for the cool evenings.

In the winter collection, Caitlin's wearing a long, dark (**7**) raincoat and black (**8**) jeans . She's also wearing black (**9**) boots on her feet.



**Vocabulary Bank** pages 90–91

# December weather

**1** **What do you usually wear in December?**

## December

It's cold and rainy outside. Winter is here in the UK. What are you wearing this month? Tell us now!

**Martin in Manchester, England:** It's raining here and it's windy too. I'm wearing my coat and I've got a new scarf. I haven't got any boots so I'm wearing trainers. My feet are cold!

**Julie and Nate in New York, USA:** It's snowy in New York. The temperature is –2°C! We're wearing jumpers, trousers, coats and very warm socks. We sometimes wear two pairs of trousers!

**Peter and Carla in Sydney, Australia:** December is summer in Australia! It's sunny here. We're sitting on the beach. I'm wearing shorts and a T-shirt. My sister's wearing a dress and sandals.

**2** ★ **Read the text. Match the names and the countries.**

| | | |
|---|---|---|
| | Nate | Australia |
| 1 | Martin | the USA |
| 2 | Carla | the UK |

**3** ★★ **Are these sentences true or false? Write T or F.**

It's snowy in Manchester. F

1. Martin isn't wearing boots. T
2. Martin's nose is cold. F
3. The temperature in New York is 2°C. F
4. Nate is wearing a warm jacket. F
5. Julie is wearing two pairs of trousers. F
6. It's hot in Sydney at the moment. T
7. Peter is swimming. F
8. Carla is wearing shorts and a T-shirt. F

**4** ★★★ **Answer the questions.**

What's the weather like in Manchester?
It's rainy and windy.

1. What's Martin wearing?
   He's wearing a coat, a scarf and trainers.
2. Why are Martin's feet cold?
   Because he's wearing trainers.
3. What's the weather like in New York?
   It's snowy and cold.
4. What are Julie and Nate wearing?
   They're wearing jumpers, trousers, coats and very warm socks.
5. What's the weather like in Sydney?
   It's sunny.
6. What are Peter and Carla doing?
   They're sitting on the beach.
7. What are they wearing?
   Peter is wearing shorts and a T-shirt. Carla is wearing a dress and sandals.

## Buying something in a shop

**1** ★ **Complete the dialogue. Use the sentences in the box.**

> ~~Can I help you?~~ Here's your change.
> How much is this scarf?
> I'd like this green scarf, please.
> That's £12.95, please.

| | |
|---|---|
| **Shop assistant** | Hello. *Can I help you?* |
| **Adam** | Yes, please. (**1**) How much is this scarf? |
| **Shop assistant** | It's £12.95. |
| **Adam** | Thank you. |
| **Adam** | (**2**) I'd like this green scarf, please. |
| **Shop assistant** | OK. (**3**) That's £12.95, please. |
| **Adam** | Here you are. |
| **Shop assistant** | Thanks. (**4**) Here's your change. |
| **Adam** | Thanks. Bye. |
| **Shop assistant** | Goodbye. |

**2** ★★ **Answer the questions.**

What is Adam looking for?
*He's looking for a scarf.*

1 How much is the scarf?
It's £12.95.

2 What colour is the scarf?
It's green.

3 What does the shop assistant give Adam?
He gives Adam his change.

**3** ★★★ **In your notebook, write a dialogue like the dialogue in exercise 1. Use the ideas in the box.**

> **item:** white T-shirt **price:** £3.99

## Dictation

**4** ★★ 4.05 **Listen. Listen again and write the sentences in your notebook.**



## Checking your spelling

**1** ★ **Choose the correct options.**

I'm **chating** / **(chatting)** to my friends.

1 I like your **(trainers)** / **traines**.
2 What's the **(weather)** / **wether** like today?
3 I've got lots of **frends** / **(friends)**.
4 Why are you **(shouting)** / **shoutting**?

**2** ★★ **Correct the spelling mistakes.**

The **temparature** is **worm** today. ✗
*temperature warm*

1 Your **cusin** is **smileing** at me. ✗
cousin smiling

2 My **geografy teecher** is very nice. ✗
geography teacher

3 This is a **beatiful foto** of your sister. ✗
beautiful photo

4 In **autum** it's **windey** in England. ✗
autumn windy

**3** ★★★ **Correct the spelling mistakes.**

In this ~~foto~~, I'm with my sister Maddy and my ~~muther~~ and father. We're on holiday and it's a ~~suny~~ day so we're ~~havving~~ fun at the beach.

I'm next to my dad. He's wearing ~~shirts~~ and a blue shirt. Maddy is next to me. She's wearing white shorts. My mum's wearing short ~~traosers~~ and a white T-shirt.

*photo*
1 mother
2 sunny
3 having
4 shorts
5 trousers


Writing Builder page 105

# 5 At home

## Vocabulary

### Parts of a house

**1** ★ **Study the picture. Match the letters and the words.**

balcony *e*

1 bathroom b
2 bedroom c
3 dining room f
4 garage h
5 garden k
6 hall j
7 kitchen d
8 living room g
9 patio l
10 stairs i
11 toilet a

**2** ★★ **Complete the crossword. Where do you find the things in the pictures?**

1

5
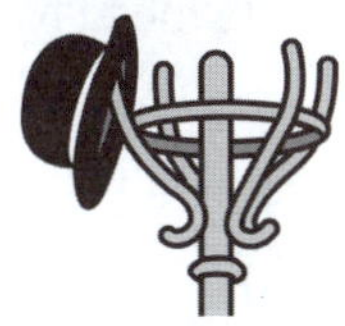

2

6

3

7

4

8

**3** ★★★ **Write true sentences about your house.**

*My house has got three bedrooms.*
*The bathroom's next to my bedroom.*

1 Students' answers
2 ______________________
3 ______________________
4 ______________________

## *there's / there are*

**1** ★ **Are these sentences affirmative, negative or interrogative? Write A, N or I.**

There isn't a bathroom on the ground floor. N

1 Is there a garden in your new house? I
2 There are two jackets in the hall. A
3 There isn't a rubber in your pencil case. N
4 There's a toilet next to the stairs. A
5 Are there any chairs on the balcony? I
6 There aren't any chairs on the balcony. N
7 Is there a good programme on TV? I
8 There are three footballs and a tennis ball in the garden. A

**2** ★★ **Complete the sentences. Use *There's*, *There are*, *There isn't* and *There aren't*.**

There isn't an English exam on Tuesday. It's on Wednesday.

1 There aren't any good films at the cinema. Let's buy a DVD.
2 There are three difficult questions in this exercise. Can you help me, please?
3 There's a blue T-shirt on the bed. Is it Jack's?
4 There are two guitars in my brother's room. Let's play.
5 There's a mobile phone on the floor. I think it's Sarah's phone.
6 There aren't any boots in your room. I can see some shoes.
7 There isn't a table in our kitchen. It's a small room.
8 There's an interesting programme on TV at six o'clock. Can I watch it?
9 There are eleven bedrooms and twelve bathrooms in that big house!

**3** ★★ **Complete the questions. Use *Is there* and *Are there*.**

Is there a maths class today?

1 Are there any shops near your house?
2 Is there a new girl in your class?
3 Are there any apples on the table?
4 Is there an exam on Friday?
5 Is there an umbrella in my bag?
6 Are there any dogs in the garden?

**4** ★★ **Write short answers for the questions in exercise 3.**

✓ Yes, there is.

1 ✗ No, there aren't.
2 ✓ Yes, there is.
3 ✓ Yes, there are.
4 ✗ No, there isn't.
5 ✓ Yes, there is.
6 ✗ No, there aren't.


Grammar Bank pages 74–75

5 ★★★ **Complete the dialogue. Use the correct forms of *there is* and *there are*.**

**Dad** What are you doing?
**Angie** I'm drawing a picture of my perfect home. It's a competition. There's an incredible computer for the best idea!
**Dad** But (1) there's ______ a computer in our living room!
**Angie** Yes, but (2) there isn't ______ a computer in my bedroom!
**Dad** So what's in your perfect home? (3) Is there ______ a kitchen?
**Angie** No, (4) there isn't ______. We buy food on the Internet. We don't cook.
**Dad** OK. (5) Is there ______ a living room?
**Angie** Yes, (6) there is ______. It's really big. (7) There are ______ three televisions. We watch TV all the time in my perfect home!
**Dad** Boring! (8) Are there ______ any bedrooms?
**Angie** Yes, (9) there are ______. (10) There are ______ six bedrooms – one for me and five for my friends. And (11) there's ______ a bathroom in each bedroom.
**Dad** Nice … but where does our family sleep?
**Angie** Oh, sorry. (12) There aren't ______ any bedrooms for you. But (13) there are ______ some enormous garages! Perhaps ….
**Dad** Angie!

# Imperative

6 ★ **Choose the correct options.**

**(Get up!)** / **Don't get up!** We're going out!

1 **(Don't open)** / **Open** the window. It's really windy.
2 **(Put)** / **Don't put** your hand on my head. Is it hot?
3 **(Come)** / **Don't come** to Computer Club. It's fun!
4 **Invite** / **(Don't invite)** Joe to the party. I don't like him.
5 **Speak** / **(Don't speak)** Spanish! It's an English class.

7 ★★ **Complete the sentences. Use affirmative or negative imperative forms of the verbs in the box.**

| be ~~listen~~ play stand up use wear |
|---|

Listen! This is interesting.

1 Use ______ my computer. It's really fast.
2 Don't play ______ football in the house!
3 Be ______ quiet! Mum is sleeping.
4 Don't wear ______ sandals. It's raining outside.
5 Stand up ______, Maisie. We can't see you.

8 ★★★ **Read the sentences. Write your responses. Use the imperative and your own ideas.**

Your brother is using your computer. He didn't ask you.
✓ Ask me before you use my computer!

1 Your dad is watching TV. It's sunny outside.
✓ Students' answers ______
2 The film starts at eight o'clock. Your friend is often late.
✗ ______
3 Your friend is reading a book. You know it's a boring book.
✗ ______
4 Your friend is wearing a T-shirt. It's cold.
✓ ______

## Furniture

**1** ★ **Choose the correct options. Use the pictures.**

(wardrobe) / lamp

1 (bookcase) / shelf

2 armchair / (sofa)

3 fridge / (cooker)

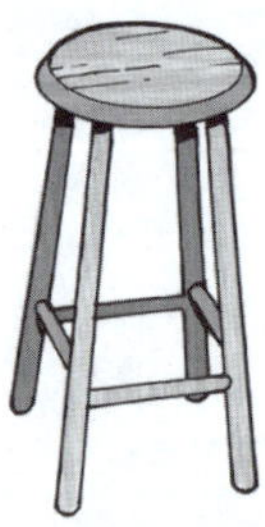

4 (stool) / mirror

5 sink / (bath)

6 bedside table / (chest of drawers)

**2** ★★ **Complete the puzzle. Use the pictures.**

| | | | | | | | | | | | | |
|---|---|---|---|---|---|---|---|---|---|---|---|---|
| | b | e | d | s | i | d | e | t | a | b | l | e |
| 1 | | | s | i | n | k | | | | | | |
| 2 | | | | b | a | t | h | | | | | |
| 3 | a | r | m | c | h | a | i | r | | | | |
| 4 | m | i | r | r | o | r | | | | | | |
| 5 | | | | c | u | p | b | o | a | r | d | |
| 6 | | | | | s | o | f | a | | | | |
| 7 | c | o | o | k | e | r | | | | | | |

4

1

5

2

6

3

7

**3** ★★★ **Write true sentences about furniture in your house.**

In my living room, there's *a sofa and there are two armchairs.*

1 In my kitchen, there *Students' answers* ______________________.

2 In my bedroom, there ______________________.

3 In my bathroom, there ______________________.



**Vocabulary Bank** pages 92–93

# My favourite room

**1 What's your favourite part of your house?**

There isn't a place to sit in my favourite room. It's our bathroom. There are just two things: a bath and a sink. And I love it! I have a bath every evening and it's really quiet – just me and our cat!

*Hardeep*

My favourite part of the house isn't a room. It's our balcony! It's usually sunny here. I play the guitar here and I sleep in the armchair. I listen to the people in the street under me. I love that.

*Stephen*

Come in! This is the BEST room in our house. My friends always sit in here. There's a TV and a computer and there are two beds. There's only one problem. My sister sleeps here too!

*Ruby*

a)

b)

**2 ★ Read the text. Match the names and the photos.**

Hardeep b)

1 Stephen c)

2 Ruby a)

**3 ★★ Are these sentences true or false? Write T or F.**

There aren't any chairs in Hardeep's bathroom. T

1 Hardeep has a bath after he gets up in the morning. F

2 Hardeep's cat likes his bathroom. T

3 There's an armchair on Stephen's balcony. T

4 Stephen likes listening to people in the street. T

5 Stephen plays the piano. F

6 Ruby can't watch TV in her bedroom. F

7 Ruby and her sister sleep in the same room. T

**4 ★★★ Answer the questions.**

Is there a chair in Hardeep's bathroom?
No, there isn't. There isn't a place to sit.

1 How often does Hardeep have a bath?
He has a bath every evening.

2 Why does he like the bathroom?
Because it's really quiet.

3 What does Stephen do on the balcony?
He plays the guitar and sleeps and listens to people in the street.

4 What can Ruby do in her bedroom?
She can watch TV and she can use a computer.

5 Why has Ruby got two beds in her bedroom?
Because her sister sleeps in the same room.

c)

## Making a phone call

**1** ★ **Complete the dialogue. Use the sentences in the box.**

> Bye, Mr Jones! Can I speak to Grace, please?
> Can she call you back in twenty minutes?
> ~~Hello.~~ It's Evie. My number is 724 8069.

| | |
|---|---|
| **Mr Jones** | Hello. |
| **Evie** | Hi, Mr Jones. **(1)** It's Evie. |
| **Mr Jones** | Hello, Evie. How are you? |
| **Evie** | I'm fine, thanks. **(2)** Can I speak to Grace, please? |
| **Mr Jones** | I'm sorry. She's having dinner at the moment. **(3)** Can she call you back in twenty minutes? |
| **Evie** | Of course. **(4)** My number is 724 8069. |
| **Mr Jones** | 724 8069. OK. Bye, Evie! |
| **Evie** | **(5)** Bye, Mr Jones! |

**2** ★★ **Answer the questions.**

Who is Evie speaking to?
She's speaking to Grace's dad.

1 How is Evie?
She's fine.

2 Who does Evie want to speak to?
She wants to speak to Grace.

3 What is Evie's friend doing?
She's having dinner.

4 When can Evie's friend call her back?
In twenty minutes.

5 What is Evie's phone number?
It's 724 8069.

**3** ★★★ **In your notebook, write a dialogue like the dialogue in exercise 1. Your friend is doing homework.**

## Dictation

**4** ★★ 4.06 **Listen. Listen again and write the sentences in your notebook.**



## *and* and *but*

**1** ★ **Choose the correct options.**

It's sunny **and** / **(but)** it's cold.

1 It's windy **(and)** / **but** it's rainy.

2 There's a sofa **and** / **(but)** there aren't any armchairs.

3 She often wears skirts **and** / **(but)** she never wears dresses.

4 Tom likes history **(and)** / **but** he's very good at it.

**2** ★★ **Connect the sentences. Use *and* or *but*.**

There's a computer. There isn't a TV.
There's a computer but there isn't a TV.

1 In the bathroom, there's a bath. There's a shower.
In the bathroom, there's a bath and there's a shower.

2 I like music. I can't sing.
I like music but I can't sing.

3 My dad has breakfast. He almost never has lunch.
My dad has breakfast but he almost never has lunch.

4 At school we play football. We do athletics.
At school we play football and we do athletics.

5 We've got a balcony. We haven't got a garden.
We've got a balcony but we haven't got a garden.

**3** ★★★ **Complete the description. Use your own ideas.**

We live in a house in Cardiff, Wales. I live with my parents and two brothers. I've got a sister but she doesn't live at home. She's at university.

We always eat in the kitchen and **(1)** Students' answers ________. We watch TV in the living room but **(2)** ________. There's also a computer room on the ground floor and **(3)** ________.

On the first floor there are three bedrooms and **(4)** ________. I don't share my bedroom but **(5)** ________.


Writing Builder page 106

# 6 Are you hungry?

## Vocabulary

### Breakfast

**1** ★ **Match the sentences and the pictures.**

1 Clare has cereal with milk. l), g)
2 Simon has yoghurt, fruit and apple juice. h), c), a)
3 Alex has bread and jam. f), e)
4 Sam has bacon and eggs. d), k)
5 Alison has toast, butter and honey. j), i), b)

a) 

g) 

b) 

h) 

c) 

i) 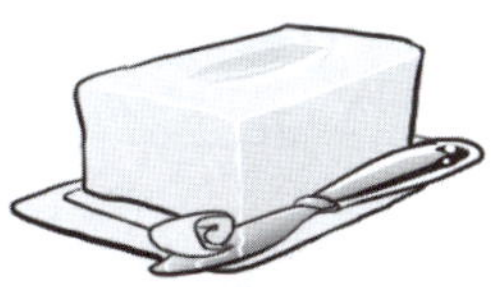

d) 

j) 

e) 

k) 

f) 

l) 

**2** ★★ **Complete the crossword.**

| | | | | | | | | |
|---|---|---|---|---|---|---|---|---|
| | | 1 B | U | T | T | 2 E | R | |
| | | | | | | G | | |
| | | | | | | G | | |
| | | 3 C | H | E | E | S | E | |
| | | E | | | | | | |
| | 4 F | R | U | I | 5 T | | | |
| 6 J | | E | | | O | | | |
| A | | A | | 7 B | A | C | O | N |
| 8 M | I | L | K | | S | | | |
| | | | | | T | | | |

1 You put this on bread or toast.
2 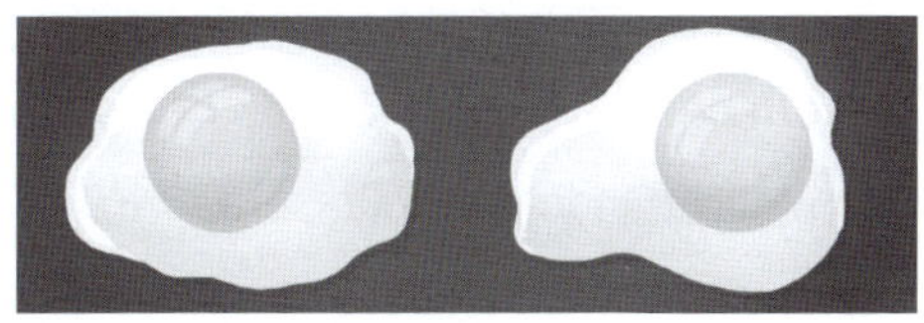
3 → This comes from milk.
3 ↓ You eat this with milk for breakfast.
4 Apples, oranges and bananas are examples of this.
5 You make this with bread.
6 You put this on bread or toast.
7 This comes from a: 
8 This is a white drink.

**3** ★★★ **Complete the text.**

I love breakfast. It's my favourite meal. On weekdays I have some *cereal* with (**1**) milk. I also have some orange (**2**) juice to drink. Then I have some (**3**) toast / bread and I usually put (**4**) butter / jam / honey on it. Finally, I always have some (**5**) fruit – maybe an apple or a banana. At weekends my dad cooks breakfast. We have bacon and (**6**) eggs.

## Countable and uncountable nouns

**1** ★ **Are these nouns countable or uncountable? Write C or U.**

bread U

1 baked beans C
2 milk U
3 bacon U
4 tomato C
5 cereal U
6 apple C
7 butter U
8 orange juice U

**2** ★★ **Some of these sentences are not complete. Complete them. Use *a* or *an*.**

Can I have an orange, please?
**or**
I love __ bacon. ✓

1 We're having __ baked beans on toast. ✓
2 I'd like a smoothie, please.
3 Is this an English sausage?
4 We'd like __ four apples, please. ✓
5 I drink __ orange juice every day. ✓
6 Do you want a biscuit with your coffee?
7 Martin doesn't eat __ peanuts. ✓
8 I want an egg for breakfast.

**3** ★★★ **Complete true sentences. Use countable and uncountable nouns.**

At breakfast, I sometimes eat two eggs.
I often drink milk.

1 On toast, I like Students' answers ________.
2 In sandwiches, I usually have ________ ________.
3 At lunch, I usually have ________ ________.
4 At dinner, I usually drink ________ ________.
5 I never drink ________.

## *some* and *any*

**4** ★ **Choose the correct options.**

We haven't got **some** / **any** bread.

1 My sister wants **some** / **any** milk.
2 Are there **some** / **any** tomatoes in the fridge?
3 Have you got **some** / **any** baked beans?
4 I'd like **some** / **any** butter on my toast.
5 You haven't got **some** / **any** apples.
6 Have we got **some** / **any** orange juice?
7 I'd like **some** / **any** biscuits, please.
8 Isabel doesn't want **some** / **any** cereal.

**5** ★★ **Complete the dialogue. Use *some* or *any*.**

**Sam** What are we having after dinner?
**Chloe** Well, there's some yoghurt.
**Sam** Yoghurt? I can make **(1)** some ________ fruit salad. Have we got **(2)** any ________ bananas?
**Chloe** Yes, we have. There are **(3)** some ________ bananas on the table.
**Sam** Are there **(4)** any ________ oranges?
**Chloe** No, but there are **(5)** some ________ kiwis in the fridge.
**Sam** Is there **(6)** any ________ orange juice?
**Chloe** Yes. Good idea. You can put **(7)** some ________ orange juice in the fruit salad.
**Sam** OK. Let's start!


Grammar Bank pages 76–77

**6** ★★★ **Think about your kitchen cupboards and your fridge. Write true sentences. Use *some* or *any* and the words in brackets.**

(jam)
There is some jam.
**or** There isn't any jam.

**or**

(eggs)
We've got some eggs.
**or** We haven't got any eggs.

1 (jam) There Students' answers ______.
2 (honey) We ______.
3 (oranges) There ______.
4 (cola) We ______.
5 (cheese) There ______.
6 (biscuits) We ______.
7 (bacon) There ______.
8 (baked beans) We ______.

## Indefinite pronouns

**7** ★ **Choose the correct options.**

Is there **anyone** / **anything** inside the box?
1 There isn't **something** / **anything** to eat and I'm hungry!
2 Is there **someone** / **anyone** at home?
3 There isn't **anyone** / **someone** at school! Where are they?
4 There's **someone** / **something** on the table for you.
5 There's **someone** / **anything** in the toilet.
6 I'm bored. There isn't **anything** / **anyone** on TV.
7 There's **anything** / **something** under your bed.
8 Is there **anything** / **anyone** for breakfast?

**8** ★★ **Complete the dialogue. Use *someone, anyone, something* or *anything*.**

**Dad** Sara! Listen! There's someone in the house.
**Mum** There isn't (**1**) anyone in the house. Go to sleep.
**Dad** I'm going downstairs. There's (**2**) someone in the living room. I can hear people.
**Dad** Hello? Is there (**3**) anyone downstairs?
**Mark** Yes, Dad. It's me. I don't want to go to bed. There's (**4**) something good on TV.
**Dad** It's three o'clock in the morning! There isn't (**5**) anything good on TV at this time. Ah! Football! You can watch it tomorrow.
**Mark** OK, Dad. Sorry.
**Dad** Don't worry. Is there (**6**) anything you want before I go to bed?
**Mark** Yes, there is. I'd like a TV in my room.
**Dad** Mark! Go to bed!

**9** ★★★ **Complete the sentences. Use the correct forms of *there is* and *there are* and indefinite pronouns.**

'There isn't anything to eat.' ✗
'I know. I'm going to the shops today.'

1 'Is there anyone in the classroom?' **?**
'Yes, our teacher.'
2 'Mum! There's someone in the house.' ✓
'It's Dad. He's working at home today.'
3 'Is there anything you want from the fridge?' **?**
'Yes, please. Can I have some milk?'
4 'There isn't anyone in the café.' ✗
'No, I think everyone's at the park.'
5 'There's something in my water.' ✓
'It's a little insect. Get some more water from the sink.'

## Lunch and dinner

**1** ★ **Find the words. Then match the words and the pictures.**

| | | | | | | | | | |
|---|---|---|---|---|---|---|---|---|---|
| H | D | G | A | A | S | U | K | I | A |
| F | S | F | R | H | T | G | G | R | G |
| P | U | W | C | A | R | R | O | T | S |
| C | B | A | E | M | A | E | H | U | A |
| H | H | W | C | B | W | S | B | R | N |
| I | H | C | N | U | B | R | F | C | D |
| C | D | C | R | R | E | R | E | A | W |
| K | H | F | P | G | R | B | N | U | I |
| E | R | I | C | E | R | R | S | P | C |
| N | D | S | P | R | I | I | E | U | H |
| K | S | H | G | S | E | F | R | R | E |
| T | S | A | E | B | S | E | H | C | S |

strawberries

4 fish

1 hamburgers

5 sandwiches

2 chips

6 rice

3 carrots

7 chicken

**2** ★★ **Correct the mistakes.**

Can I have a **salad green**, please? ✗
*Can I have green salad, please?*

1 Have we got any **potatos**? ✗
Have we got any potatoes?

2 Can I have a hamburger and **chip**, please? ✗
Can I have a hamburger and chips, please?

3 This is a good **cake chocolate**. ✗
This is a good chocolate cake.

4 I don't like **rices** with chicken. ✗
I don't like rice with chicken.

5 We often have **beef roast** on Sundays. ✗
We often have roast beef on Sundays.

**3** ★★★ **Complete the quiz.**

### 10 questions about food

**Answer the ten questions in three minutes!**

1 Name a red fruit. *strawberries*

2 Name an orange vegetable. carrots

3 What food do you buy in fast food restaurants? hamburgers / fish / chips

4 Name a green vegetable. peas

5 What do you use to make chips? potatoes

6 What food comes from the sea? fish

7 Which white food do you use to make paella? rice / fish

8 What can you make from bread, butter and cheese? A cheese sandwich.

9 What food do Italians eat a lot? pasta / ice cream

10 Find the food: cie racem. ice cream


Vocabulary Bank pages 94–95

# School lunches

**1 What do you eat for lunch on a school day?**

## School food around the world

At twelve o'clock our class has lunch. We haven't got a school canteen. In Japan, we eat in the classroom. Today it's fish or chicken with rice. My friends bring packed lunches. After lunch we clean the classroom.

*Akane*

Today we're having salad, then roast chicken and carrots, then cheese and then cake! We always drink water. There's a fast food restaurant near our school but there isn't anyone in it. French school meals are great!

*Pascal*

Schools in Norway almost never serve lunch. Everyone brings a packed lunch. I often have a sandwich with cheese or roast beef and some fruit. You can buy milk or yoghurt at school. We only have 30 minutes for lunch.

*Lars*

**2 ★ Read the text. Match the names and the countries.**

| | | |
|---|---|---|
| | Akane | Norway |
| 1 | Pascal | Japan |
| 2 | Lars | France |

**3 ★★ Are these sentences true or false? Write T or F.**

Akane has lunch in her classroom. T

1 Today she's having a packed lunch. F
2 After lunch, Akane and her friends clean the classroom. T
3 Lots of children go to the fast food restaurant near Pascal's school. F
4 In Norway, children bring lunch to school. T
5 You can buy something to drink at Lars's school. T

**4 ★★★ Answer the questions.**

Where does Akane have lunch?
She has lunch in her classroom.

1 What does Akane do after lunch?
She cleans the classroom.
2 What is Pascal having for lunch today?
He's having salad, roast chicken and carrots, cheese and cake.
3 Why don't people go to the fast food restaurant near Pascal's school?
Because French school meals are great.
4 What do schools sell in Norway?
They sell milk and yoghurt.
5 How long is lunchtime at Lars's school?
It's 30 minutes.

## Ordering food

**1 ★ Complete the dialogue. Use the sentences and phrases in the box.**

And for you? And to drink? Anything else? ~~Can I take your order?~~ Have you got I'd like

| | |
|---|---|
| **Waiter** | Hello. *Can I take your order?* |
| **Sam** | (1) I'd like roast beef with potatoes, please. |
| **Waiter** | And to drink? |
| **Sam** | Water, please. |
| **Waiter** | OK. (2) And for you? |
| **Dan** | I'd like chicken and chips, please. |
| **Waiter** | (3) And to drink? |
| **Dan** | (4) Have you got any cola? |
| **Waiter** | Yes, we have. (5) Anything else? |
| **Dan** | No, thank you. |

**2 ★★ Complete the chart with the food and drinks that Sam and Dan order.**

| | food | drink |
|---|---|---|
| Sam | *roast beef with potatoes* | (2) water |
| Dan | (1) chicken and chips | (3) cola |

**3 ★★★ In your notebook, write a dialogue like the dialogue in exercise 1. Use the menu.**

CATE'S CAFÉ

**Snacks £5**
sandwiches (roast beef, chicken, bacon, cheese)
hamburger

**Drinks £2**
cola
juice (orange, apple)

**Side dishes £2**
chips
rice
green salad

**Desserts £3**
ice cream
chocolate cake

## Dictation

**4 ★★ 4.07 Listen. Listen again and write the sentences in your notebook.**



## Using paragraphs

**1 ★ There are four paragraphs. Write 1 to 4 where the paragraphs start.**

*1* My favourite restaurant is Tina's in Oxford. It's only open at lunchtime. 2 At Tina's, they're famous for their hamburgers. They're fantastic! They've also got great sausages. 3 There are also some great desserts at Tina's. I always have banana cake. 4 I think Tina's is a great restaurant. The food and desserts are great.

**2 ★★ Match the sentences and the paragraphs from exercise 1.**

a) We sometimes go there on Sundays. *1*
b) My best friend loves the honey ice cream. 3
c) The people are nice too! 4
d) They've got very good pasta too. 2

**3 ★★★ Complete the description of Lara's favourite restaurant. Use the notes.**

*Name? The Pizza Place, Italian restaurant*
*How often? Sometimes on Saturday evenings*
*Food? Famous for pizza, but also serves pasta, Italian sausages*
*Desserts? Only one, ice cream, but 30 different types! Me – always chocolate*

a) My favourite restaurant *is The Pizza Place*.
b) It's an Italian restaurant.
c) We sometimes go there on Saturday evenings.
d) The Pizza Place is famous for pizza.
e) They also serve pasta and Italian sausages.
f) They've only got one dessert.
g) It's ice cream.
h) But they've got 30 different types!
i) I always have chocolate.

**4 ★★★ Which sentences in exercise 3 must be in the same paragraph?**

1 Paragraph 1: *a)*, b), c)
2 Paragraph 2: d), e)
3 Paragraph 3: f), g), h), i)


Writing Builder page 107

# 7 Cities and towns

## Vocabulary

### Places in town (1)

**1** ★ **Choose the correct options.**

You can listen to music at a **concert hall** / **palace**.

1 You watch films at the **cinema** / **theatre**.
2 There are lots of shops at the **hospital** / **shopping centre**.
3 You watch sport at the **stadium** / **river**.
4 You can see paintings at the **museum** / **art gallery**.
5 You find aeroplanes at the **bridge** / **airport**.

**2** ★★ **Complete the words. Then match the words and parts of the picture on the right.**

museum f

1 theatre i
2 bus station j
3 stadium d
4 train station b
5 hospital e
6 cinema c
7 airport a
8 river h
9 bridge g

**3** ★★★ **Complete the sentences.**

We're going to the hospital. The baby's ill.

1 The king lives in this palace.
2 The shopping centre near my school's very big. There are 255 shops!
3 My brother often goes to the museum because he loves dinosaurs.
4 There was an amazing painting by Salvador Dali at the art gallery.

## *be*: past simple

**1** ★ **Choose the correct options.**

It (was) / **were** snowy yesterday and it was very cold!

1 The man's eyes **wasn't** / (**weren't**) brown. They were blue.
2 Kate wasn't here last week. She (**was**) / **were** in Spain.
3 The weather (**wasn't**) / **weren't** cold yesterday. It was hot!
4 We **wasn't** / (**weren't**) at school yesterday. It was Sunday!
5 There aren't any sandwiches. I (**was**) / **were** hungry.
6 These trousers **was** / (**were**) £50!
7 You **wasn't** / (**weren't**) at my party! Why?

**2** ★ **Match the questions and the answers.**

Was Mark at the cinema yesterday? *c)*
1 Were you on holiday last week? f)
2 Was I a good baby? b)
3 Was the film interesting? a)
4 Were your parents at the airport? e)
5 Were you and Beth in the same class last year? d)

a) No, it wasn't. I was bored.
b) Yes, you were. Your brother was terrible!
c) Yes, he was. I was also there.
d) No, we weren't. My teacher was Mrs Murphy.
e) Yes, they were. I was really happy to see them!
f) No, I wasn't. I was at school.

**3** ★★ **Complete Jessica's report. Use the affirmative or negative of *was* or *were*.**

Yesterday my little brother *was* at the museum with my dad. I usually go with them but they (**1**) were at the dinosaur museum. Dinosaurs are boring!

It (**2**) was sunny and I (**3**) was with some friends near the river. We (**4**) weren't in the water because it isn't good to swim there.

My mum (**5**) was at the train station. She and my grandma (**6**) were there to meet my big brother but his train (**7**) wasn't on time. It (**8**) was two hours late. My mum and my grandma (**9**) weren't happy!

**4** ★★ **Write questions and short answers. Use the text in exercise 3.**

it sunny / yesterday
*Was it sunny yesterday?*
*Yes, it was.*

1 Jessica's brother and her dad / at the museum
Were Jessica's brother and her dad at the museum?
Yes, they were.

2 Jessica / at the museum
Was Jessica at the museum?
No, she wasn't.

3 Jessica / with her friends
Was Jessica with her friends?
Yes, she was.

4 Jessica's mum and her grandma / on a train
Were Jessica's mum and her grandma on a train?
No, they weren't.

5 the train / on time
Was the train on time?
No, it wasn't.


Grammar Bank pages 78–79

**5** ★★★ **Complete the sentences. Use your own ideas.**

Last Saturday it was hot and sunny but *on Sunday it was very cold*.

1 The living room wasn't big but Students' answers ______.

2 They were at the airport on time but ______.

3 I wasn't with Tom yesterday because ______.

4 We were at the concert yesterday but ______.

5 Mr Carr wasn't here yesterday because ______.

**6** ★★★ **Write short answers. Then write questions for the answers. Use the past simple interrogative of *be*.**

(you) *Were you at the shopping centre yesterday?*
✓ *Yes, I was.* But my favourite shop was closed!

1 (the music) Was the music good?
✗ No, it wasn't. It was terrible!

2 (exam results) Were your exam results good?
✓ Yes, they were. They were all As!

3 (the weather) Was the weather good / hot / warm / sunny?
✓ Yes, it was. I was at the beach.

4 (you and your sister) Were you and your sister on time?
✗ No, we weren't. We were late!

## *there was / there were*

**7** ★ **Are these sentences correct or incorrect? Write ✓ or ✗.**

Was there any sandwiches on the menu? ✗

1 There weren't a balcony in our hotel room. ✗

2 Was there a toilet in the café? ✓

3 There was only two eggs in the fridge. ✗

4 There was a problem with the train. ✓

5 There were a big stadium near our hotel. ✗

6 There weren't any taxis. ✓

**8** ★★ **Complete the dialogue. Use the correct forms of *there was* and *there were*.**

**Dan** I was at an art gallery yesterday. *There was* an exhibition of comics.

**Joe** Really? (1) Was there anything good there?

**Dan** Yes, (2) there was. (3) There were the first *Batman* and *Spiderman* comics.

**Joe** Wow! (4) Were there any famous artists there?

**Dan** No, (5) there weren't.

**Joe** (6) Were there any comics by Spanish artists?

**Dan** Yes, (7) there were. (8) There were some drawings by Daniel Acuña. He draws the X-Men now.

**Joe** Next time, phone me! (9) There wasn't anything on TV yesterday. I was bored.

**9** ★★★ **Write true sentences about an event. Use the affirmative and the negative of *there was* and *there were*.**

I was *at a computer games party last Saturday.*
*There was some cola and some orange juice.*
*There weren't any teachers.*

1 I was at Students' answers ______.

2 ______

3 ______

4 ______

5 ______

6 ______

# Places in town (2)

**1** ★ **Find the places.**

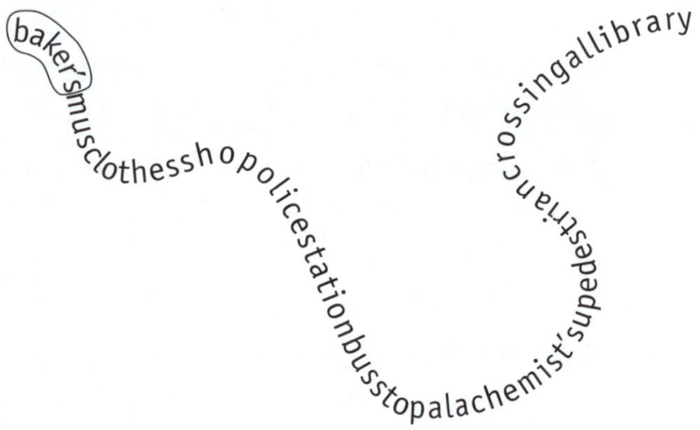


baker's
1 clothes shop
2 police station
3 bus stop
4 chemist's
5 pedestrian crossing
6 library

**2** ★★ **Complete the places. Use the pictures on the right.**

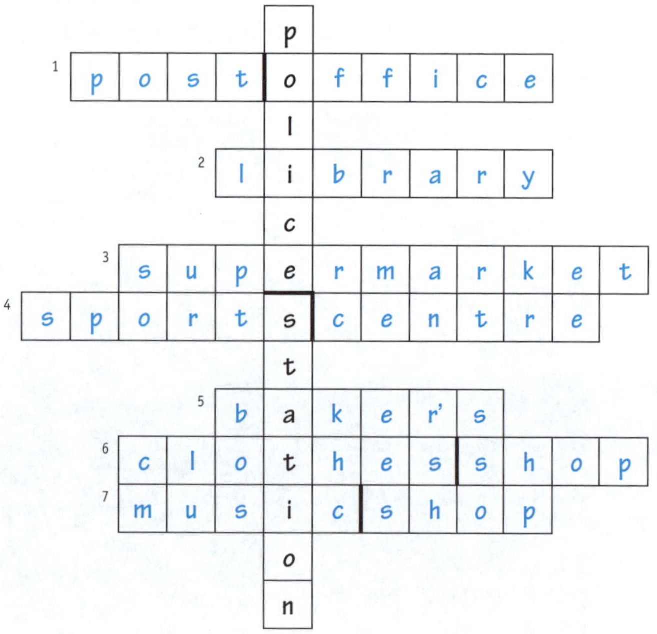


**3** ★★★ **Write definitions.**

chemist's You can buy medicine here.
1 library You can borrow books here.
2 bus stop You can wait for a bus here.
3 pedestrian crossing You can cross the road here.
4 post office You can buy stamps here.
5 police station You can talk to a police officer here.

4

1

5
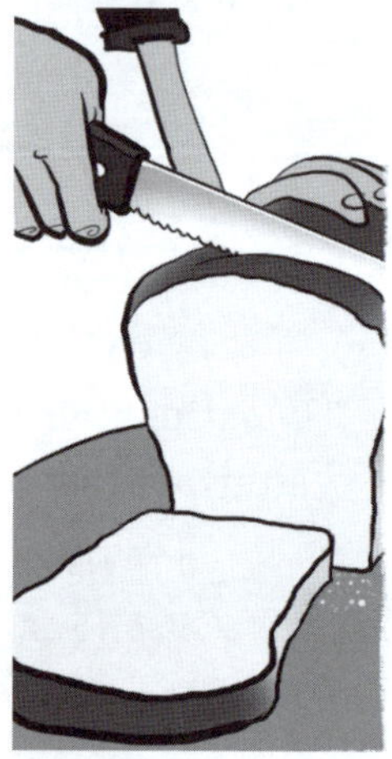

2

6

3

7

Vocabulary Bank pages 96–97

# A music festival

**1** **Are there any music festivals in your town?**

## Glastonbury Festival

Glastonbury is a town in south-west England. About 9,000 people live in Glastonbury. It's usually a quiet place.

But every summer there's a festival near the town: Glastonbury Festival. There are three days of music, comedy and fun.

The first festival was in 1970. There were 1,500 people and 16 bands. Tickets were £1 and there was free milk.

Now Glastonbury Festival is famous. There are theatres, shops, and special activities for children, and there's a lot of music! It often rains but people sleep in tents.

In 2009, Glastonbury was enormous. Two months before the festival there weren't any tickets. There were 140,000 visitors and 500 bands. Tickets were £175 ... but there wasn't any free milk!

**2** ★ **Read the text. How many bands were there at Glastonbury festival in 2009?** 500

**3** ★★ **Read the text. Complete the chart.**

| Year | Number of people | Number of bands | Price of ticket |
|---|---|---|---|
| 1970 | (2) 1,500 | (4) 16 | (6) £ 1 |
| (1) 2009 | (3) 140,000 | (5) 500 | (7) £ 175 |

**4** ★★★ **Answer the questions.**

Where is Glastonbury?
It's in south-west England.

1. How many people live in the town?
   About 9,000 people live in the town.
2. What happens every summer?
   Every summer there's a festival near the town.
3. How long is the festival for?
   The festival is for three days.
4. What was there to drink at the first Glastonbury Festival?
   There was milk.
5. Where do people sleep at Glastonbury Festival?
   People sleep in tents.
6. Do children go to the festival?
   Yes, they do. There are special activities for children.
7. Is the weather always good at Glastonbury?
   No, it isn't. It often rains.
8. How much were the tickets in 1970 and 2009?
   The tickets were £1 in 1970 and they were £175 in 2009.

## Giving directions

**1** ★ **Put the sentences in the correct order.**

| | |
|---|---|
| **Man** | Thank you. 5 |
| **Man** | How do I get there? 3 |
| **Man** | Excuse me. Is there a post office near here? 1 |
| **Naomi** | Go straight on. Then turn right. It's opposite the police station, next to the cinema. 4 |
| **Naomi** | You're welcome. 6 |
| **Naomi** | Yes, there is. There's a post office in Queen Street. 2 |

**2** ★★ **Answer the questions.**

What place does the man want to go to?
He wants to go to the post office.

1 What street is the post office in?
The post office is in Queen Street.

2 What is opposite the post office?
The police station is opposite the post office.

3 What is next to the post office?
The cinema is next to the post office.

**3** ★★★ **In your notebook, write a dialogue like the dialogue in exercise 1. Use the map.**

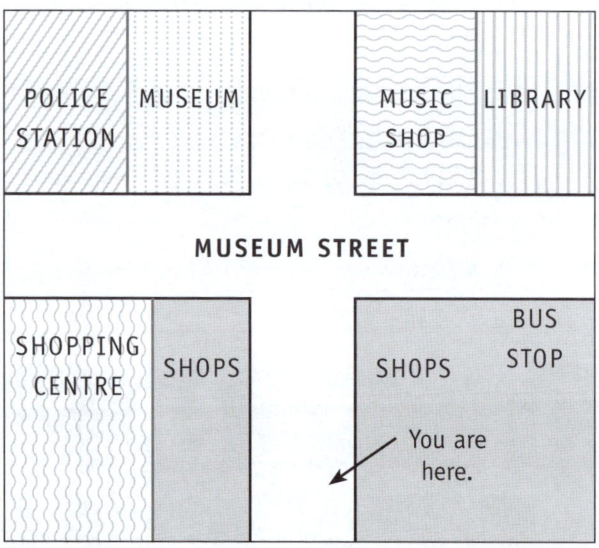


## Dictation

**4** ★★ 4.08 **Listen. Listen again and write the sentences in your notebook.**

## *also* and *too*

**1** ★ **Cross out the extra words.**

There's a sofa. There ~~also~~ is also a chair.

1 There are two cinemas. There's ~~too~~ a theatre too.

2 Jo likes museums. He ~~too~~ likes art galleries too.

3 It's cold in my town. It also rains ~~also~~ a lot.

**2** ★★ **Write sentences. Use the words in brackets.**

There's a bus station. (train station / also)
There's also a train station.

1 They sell good pasta. (great smoothies / also)
They also sell great smoothies.

2 I go to concerts. (the theatre / too)
I go to the theatre too.

3 It was a small town. (very quiet / also)
It was also very quiet.

4 She wears jeans a lot. (skirts / also)
She also wears skirts.

**3** ★★★ **Complete the email. Use the notes and *also* or *too*.**

Last week: in Edinburgh with cousin. Interesting city and the capital of Scotland. Has got Edinburgh Castle and a great palace. Has got a festival in August: music, and people go to comedy shows.

Hi Susie,

I was in Edinburgh last week. It's an interesting city and it's also the capital of Scotland. My favourite place was Edinburgh Castle. There's (**1**) also a great palace / a great palace too. In August, Edinburgh (**2**) also has a festival / has a festival too. There's music and people (**3**) also go to comedy shows / go to comedy shows too.

Write to me soon.

Morag



Writing Builder page 108

# 8 Great music

## Vocabulary

### Types of music

**1** ★ **Choose the correct options.**

Beethoven and Mozart are famous for **classical** / **jazz** music.

1 **Flamenco** / **Country** started in Andalusia.
2 Jay Z and Eminem sing **hip hop** / **gospel**.
3 José Carreras sings **opera** / **pop**.
4 **Salsa** / **Hip hop** started in Cuba.

**2** ★★ **Complete the crossword. Use the photos on the right.**

| | | | | | | | | | | | | |
|---|---|---|---|---|---|---|---|---|---|---|---|---|
| | | [1] G | O | S | [2] P | E | L | | | | | |
| | | | | | O | | | [3] O | | | | |
| | | | [4] H | I | P | [5] H | O | P | | | | |
| | | | | | | E | | E | | | | |
| [6] R | | [7] S | A | L | S | A | | R | | [8] F | | |
| O | | | | | | V | | A | | L | | |
| [9] C | O | U | N | T | R | Y | | | [10] J | A | Z | Z |
| K | | | | | | M | | | | M | | |
| | | | | | [11] R | E | G | G | A | E | | |
| | | | | | | T | | | | N | | |
| | | | | [12] C | L | A | S | S | I | C | A | L |
| | | | | | | L | | | | O | | |

**3** ★★★ **Complete true sentences about music.**

I almost never listen to *gospel*.

1 I like Students' answers but I love ________ .
2 My parents like ________ but they hate ________ .
3 My favourite English ________ group is ________ .
4 My favourite Spanish ________ group is ________ .

1

7

2

8

3

9

4

10

5

11

6

12

# Past simple affirmative (regular verbs)

**1** ★ **Complete the chart about regular past simple verbs. Use the words in the box.**

~~open~~ carry planned carried plan used opened use

| Normal | Final *e* | Final consonant + *y* | Short vowel + consonant |
|---|---|---|---|
| *open* | (2) use | (4) carry | (6) plan |
| *+ ed* | *e + d* | *y + ied* | double consonant *+ ed* |
| (1) opened | (3) used | (5) carried | (7) planned |

**2** ★ **Write the past simple forms of the verbs.**

listen *listened*

1 call called
2 stop stopped
3 study studied
4 play played
5 walk walked
6 like liked

**3** ★★ **Correct the mistakes.**

They **watchd** the concert on TV. *watched*

1 I **listenned** to the song on the Internet.
listened
2 Ruby **copyed** my homework yesterday.
copied
3 We **chated** to the singer after the concert.
chatted
4 I **invitid** my parents to our concert.
invited
5 My dad **lovd** reggae when he was young.
loved

**4** ★★ **Complete the sentences. Use the past simple affirmative of the verbs in the box.**

chat dance ~~learn~~ rain record start study visit

I *learned* to play the guitar last year.

1 The concert started at 9 p.m.
2 We visited Paul McCartney's old house on holiday.
3 I danced a lot at the party. The music was great.
4 They recorded our song on Jen's computer.
5 The singer studied at my school ten years ago.
6 We were at home on Saturday because it rained all day.
7 You chatted to the group after the concert. Were they nice?

**5** ★★★ **Write true sentences about last weekend. Use the past simple affirmative forms of the verbs in the box.**

call chat play practise study ~~watch~~

Last weekend ...
My cousin *watched a film on Sunday night.*

1 I Students' answers.
2 My parents ________.
3 My friend ________.
4 My teacher ________.
5 My mum ________.

# Past simple affirmative (irregular verbs)

**6** ★ **Are these verbs regular or irregular? Write R or I.**

preferred *R*

1 said I
2 jumped R
3 did I
4 made I
5 spoke I
6 went I
7 heard I
8 worked R
9 read I


Grammar Bank pages 80–81

**7** ★★ **Write the past simple of these verbs.**

begin *began*
1 buy bought
2 meet met
3 go went
4 be was/were
5 put put
6 sing sang
7 stand stood
8 wear wore

**8** ★★ **Complete the text. Use the past simple affirmative of the verbs in exercise 7.**

Last Sunday I *went* to a music festival. I **(1)** met my best friend, Paula, at the festival. I **(2)** wore my Coldplay T-shirt. Coldplay's concert **(3)** began at 4 p.m. We **(4)** stood at the front and we **(5)** sang all the songs.

After the concert, I **(6)** bought a poster of the concert. I **(7)** put it on my bedroom wall. It **(8)** was a great day!

**9** ★★★ **Complete the text. Use the past simple affirmative of irregular verbs.**

We *saw* a U2 concert last year. We **(1)** won tickets to the concert in a competition. We **(2)** stood/sat at the front. The person next to me **(3)** paid €200 for their ticket! I also **(4)** chatted to the group after the concert. They **(5)** gave me a U2 DVD. The concert **(6)** began at 7 p.m. and we **(7)** were home at one o'clock in the morning. I **(8)** went to bed and I **(9)** slept for ten hours!

# Adverbs of manner

**10** ★ **Choose the correct options.**

This chair is very **comfortable** / **comfortably**.
1 You can play the guitar **good** / **well**.
2 I hate heavy metal music. It's very **loud** / **loudly**.
3 Can you talk **quiet** / **quietly**, please?
4 Last night I slept **terrible** / **terribly**.
5 This is an **easy** / **easily** exercise.

**11** ★★ **Complete the sentences. Use the adjectives in brackets, or adverbs formed from the adjectives in brackets.**

I think Shakira sings *wonderfully*. (wonderful)
I think Shakira is a *wonderful* singer. (wonderful)
1 He sings very fast and I can't understand the words. (fast)
2 I like his voice. He speaks very nicely. (nice)
3 Was your answer to number 10 correct? (correct)
4 We understood the Spanish children because they spoke slowly. (slow)
5 Go straight on. The music shop is on the left. (straight)
6 We saw some terrible groups at the festival. (terrible)

**12** ★★★ **Complete the sentences. Use adverbs of manner.**

1 My dad sings *terribly*! He sings in the kitchen and I always leave the room quickly.
2 Last night our team played very badly. We lost the match 4–0. After the fourth goal, our fans shouted at us loudly.
3 Simon's team did very well in the quiz. They answered all ten questions correctly.
4 I love her novels. I always read them very fast. She writes well/wonderfully.

# Musical instruments

**1 ★ Find the words. Then match the words and the photos.**

| | | | | | | | | | | |
|---|---|---|---|---|---|---|---|---|---|---|
| t | c | e | l | l | g | u | t | a | r | t |
| a | s | x | y | l | o | u | r | a | a | r |
| h | a | y | v | i | o | l | i | n | a | u |
| a | a | t | r | u | g | p | a | t | a | m |
| g | t | r | o | m | b | o | n | e | a | d |
| h | a | u | p | g | u | i | g | f | a | r |
| f | l | m | v | s | c | e | l | l | o | u |
| a | r | p | g | i | n | g | e | u | l | m |
| b | c | e | l | a | o | u | r | t | l | s |
| g | u | t | r | o | m | b | o | n | c | e |

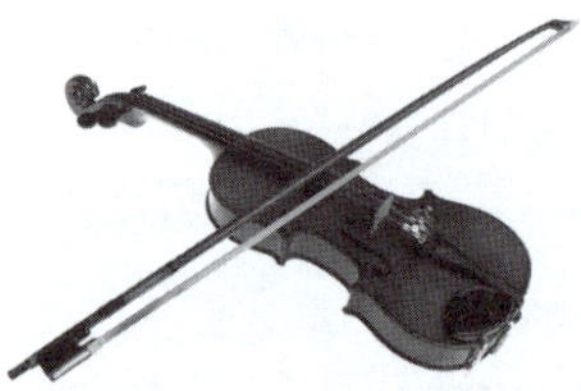

violin

4 harp

1 cello

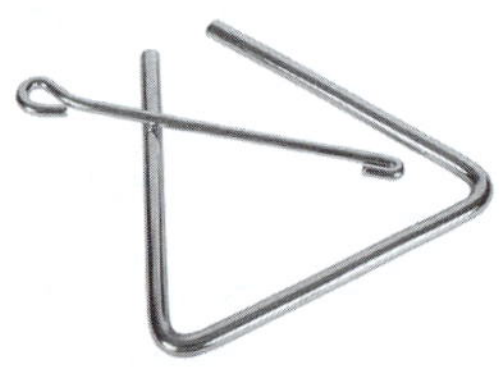

5 triangle

2 drums

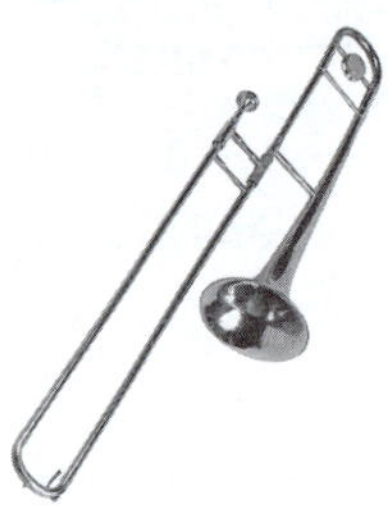

6 trombone

3 guitar

7 trumpet

**2 ★★ Write the words. Then match the words and the pictures.**

| | | | |
|---|---|---|---|
| | urigta | guitar | c) |
| 1 | rahp | harp | b) |
| 2 | etluf | flute | h) |
| 3 | cernalit | clarinet | a) |
| 4 | sbalycm | cymbals | d) |
| 5 | neopashox | saxophone | g) |
| 6 | xyonlepoh | xylophone | e) |
| 7 | mnbarueiot | tambourine | f) |

a)

e)

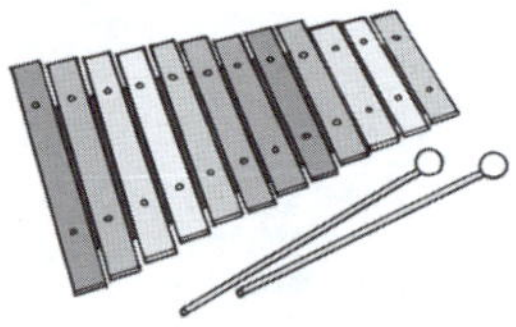

b)

f)

c)

g)

d)

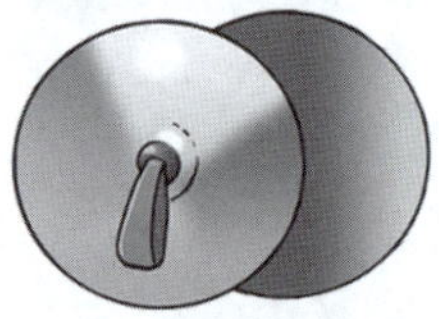

h)

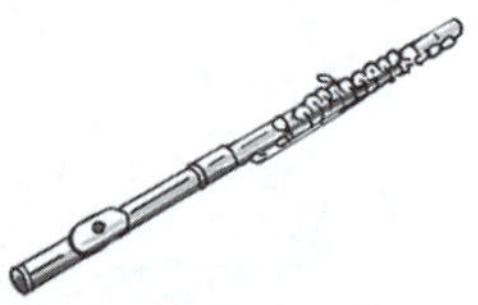

**3 ★★★ Write true answers.**

What instruments does your school teach?

*My school teaches the piano and the violin.*

1 Name two wind instruments.

Students' answers

2 Name two string instruments.

3 Name two percussion instruments.

4 What instruments can you, your family or your friends play?

5 What instruments do you want to play?


Vocabulary Bank pages 98–99

# Music shopping

**1 Have you got a T-shirt or a poster of your favourite group or singer?**

Nowadays musicians sell more than T-shirts and posters!

My parents love Johnny Cash. He was a country music singer. I was nine months old when they went to a Johnny Cash concert. They bought a Johnny Cash T-shirt. Was it for me? No, it was for our dog! **Martin**

I've got a computer game about the Beatles. You can sing rock songs and play the guitar or drums with the group. It's fantastic. The company worked on the game for three years! **Fern**

My dad loves reggae. Eleven years ago I was a baby. He bought me Bob Marley socks! I wore them when I learned to walk. There was the title of a Bob Marley song on them – 'One Love'. **Rita**

**2 ★ Read the text. Match the singers and the types of music.**

Johnny Cash – country
1 Beatles – rock
2 Bob Marley – reggae

reggae
rock
country

**3 ★★ Are these sentences true or false? Write T or F.**

Johnny Cash was a reggae singer. F
1 Martin went to the Johnny Cash concert. F
2 Martin's parents bought him a T-shirt. F
3 You can play three instruments with the Beatles game. F
4 Fern likes the game. T
5 'One Love' is a song by Bob Marley. T
6 Rita's dad bought her a Bob Marley CD. F

**4 ★★★ Complete the sentences.**

When Martin's parents went to a Johnny Cash concert, he was nine months old.
1 Martin's dog got a Johnny Cash T-shirt.
2 Fern's got a computer game about the Beatles.
3 Fern thinks it's fantastic.
4 It took three years to make the game.
5 Eleven years ago Rita's dad bought her Bob Marley socks.
6 'One Love' is a Bob Marley song.

## Making suggestions

**1 ★ Complete the dialogue. Use the phrases in the box.**

| | | |
|---|---|---|
| It's fantastic | ~~Let's buy a~~ | Shall we |
| That's a great idea | We can't | Why don't we get |

**Adam** It's Joe's birthday on Saturday. *Let's buy* *a present for him.*
**Clare** OK. (1) *Why don't we get* Jay Z's new CD? (2) *It's fantastic*!
**Adam** (3) *We can't*. Joe bought it last week.
**Clare** OK. (4) *Shall we* get a Jay Z T-shirt?
**Adam** (5) *That's a great idea*!

**2 ★★ Answer the questions.**

Who are Adam and Clare talking about?
*They're talking about their friend, Joe.*

1 When is their friend's birthday?
*On Saturday.*

2 What does Adam want to do?
*Adam wants to buy a present for Joe.*

3 What does Clare think of Jay Z's new CD?
*She thinks it's fantastic.*

4 Why do they choose something different?
*Joe bought Jay Z's new CD last week.*

5 What is Clare's second idea for a present?
*A Jay Z T-shirt.*

6 What does Adam think of Clare's second idea?
*He thinks it's a great idea.*

**3 ★★★ In your notebook, write a dialogue like the dialogue in exercise 1. Use the ideas in the box.**

| | |
|---|---|
| Shakira's new CD | a Shakira poster |

## Dictation

**4 ★★ 4.09 Listen. Listen again and write the sentences in your notebook.**

## Checking your grammar

**1 ★ Choose the correct options.**

**Does** / (**Do**) your friends go to music festivals?

1 Simon and I **am** / (**are**) listening to music.
2 He ran very (**fast**) / **fastly**.
3 We (**studied**) / **studyed** for the exam last weekend.
4 (**Have you**) / **You have** got a brother?
5 My cousin **play** / (**plays**) the cello.

**2 ★★ Correct the mistakes.**

The first two groups was terrible.
*The first two groups were terrible.*

1 I'm writting an email at the moment.
*I'm writing an email at the moment.*

2 Natalie singed a song at the concert last week.
*Natalie sang a song at the concert last week.*

3 Your brother sings very good.
*Your brother sings very well.*

4 We haven't got some U2 CDs.
*We haven't got any U2 CDs.*

5 I didn't watched TV yesterday.
*I didn't watch TV yesterday.*

**3 ★★★ Correct the mistakes.**

Beyoncé Knowles is an American singer from Texas, USA. She ~~becomed~~ famous with the group Destiny's Child.

She ~~makes~~ her first album in 2003. She had a big hit with 'Crazy in Love' with the hip hop singer Jay-Z and she ~~winned~~ five Grammy Awards in 2004. She ~~sings sometimes~~ in Spanish but she can't ~~speaks~~ the language very ~~good~~.

In 2005, she started a charity, the Survivor Foundation. In the first year, she ~~gaved~~ the charity $250,000.

*became*
1 *made*
2 *won*
3 *sometimes sings*
4 *speak*
5 *well*
6 *gave*

 Writing Builder page 109

# 9 Around the world

## Vocabulary

### Packing for a holiday

**1** ★ **Find the words.**

tentowelmapassporttorchsleepingbaguidebooksuncreammatches

tent

1 towel
2 map
3 passport
4 torch
5 sleeping bag
6 guidebook
7 suncream
8 matches

**3** ★★★ **Complete the text.**

My friend Dan packed his bag for our camping holiday in Huelva in Spain … three weeks before the holiday!

He borrowed a *guidebook* from the library and read it carefully. He bought a big (**1**) tent for us to sleep in and a (**2**) sleeping bag for the cold nights. His dad gave him a (**3**) map because he often gets lost.

He loves swimming so he packed his (**4**) swimsuit and a (**5**) towel for the beach.

He bought some expensive (**6**) suncream because he's got fair skin and Spain's hot in August. He even got a new (**7**) torch so we could see at night.

We arrived at the airport and suddenly Dan screamed. He didn't have his (**8**) passport !

**2** ★★ **Complete the puzzle and find the mystery word. Use the photos.**

| | | | | | | | | 8 | | | | |
|---|---|---|---|---|---|---|---|---|---|---|---|---|
| | | | | | p | a | s | s | p | o | r | t |
| | | | | | | | | u | | | | |
| 1 | | | | | | t | e | n | t | | | |
| 2 | s | l | e | e | p | i | n | g | b | a | g | |
| 3 | | | | t | o | w | e | l | | | | |
| 4 | | | | | | | m | a | p | | | |
| 5 | | m | a | t | c | h | e | s | | | | |
| 6 | | | | s | w | i | m | s | u | i | t | |
| 7 | | | | | c | a | m | e | r | a | | |
| | | | | | | | | s | | | | |

1

2

3

4
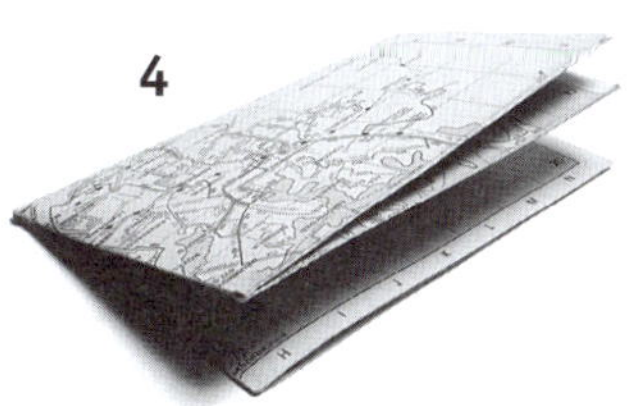

5

6

7

8 ???

## *going to*

**1 ★ Put the words in the correct order.**

practise / my English on holiday. / I'm / going to

I'm going to practise my English on holiday.

1 buy / going to / We're / a guidebook at the weekend.

We're going to buy a guidebook at the weekend.

2 going to / not / I'm / my passport. / forget

I'm not going to forget my passport.

3 going to / you / a torch? / Are / take

Are you going to take a torch?

4 in a hotel. / My aunt / going to / stay / isn't

My aunt isn't going to stay in a hotel.

5 Is it / rain / next week? / going to

Is it going to rain next week?

**2 ★★ Complete the sentences. Use the affirmative or negative of *going to* and the verbs in the box.**

be buy miss not take not write sleep ~~stay~~

I'm going to stay with my cousins in August. ✓

1 My grandparents are going to sleep in a tent! ✓

2 I 'm not going to take my camera. ✗

3 You 're going to miss the plane! ✓

4 Jen is going to buy a new sleeping bag later. ✓

5 It 's going to be a hot day tomorrow. ✓

6 Nick isn't going to write any postcards on holiday. ✗

**3 ★★ Write questions and short answers about Mo and Andy and Sue's holidays in Spain. Use *going to*.**

| | Mo | Andy and Sue |
|---|---|---|
| travel by aeroplane | ✗ | ✓ |
| visit Barcelona | ✓ | ✗ |

Is Mo going to travel by aeroplane?
No, he isn't.

1 Is Mo going to visit Barcelona?

Yes, he is.

2 Are Andy and Sue going to travel by aeroplane?

Yes, they are.

3 Are Andy and Sue going to visit Barcelona?

No, they aren't.

**4 ★★★ Study the example. Write true sentences about holiday plans.**

I'm going to visit England but I'm not going to stay in London.

1 I Students' answers ____________.

2 My best friend ____________.

3 Our teacher ____________.

4 My cousins ____________.

5 My grandparents ____________.

**5 ★★★ Write questions and complete the short answers. Use *going to*.**

Are you going to buy a guidebook?
No, I'm not. I never buy guidebooks.

1 Are they going to visit Spain next month?

No, they aren't. They visited Spain last year.

2 Is Tom going to take suncream?

No, he isn't. Tom never takes suncream.

3 Are you going to wear jeans on the plane?

Yes, I am. I always wear jeans when I travel.


Grammar Bank pages 82–83

## Present continuous with future meaning

**6** ★ **Complete the sentences. Use the notes and the affirmative or negative present continuous of the verbs in brackets.**

Holiday plan (A = Alex, T = Tom)

| | |
|---|---|
| Thursday | A: Buy food<br>T: Borrow tent from Joe |
| Friday | A and T: Catch train<br>T: Cook dinner |
| Saturday | A and T: Meet Paul at campsite |
| Sunday | A: Make sandwiches<br>A and T: Go windsurfing |
| Monday | A and T: Come home |

On Thursday, Alex **is buying** some food. (buy)

1 On Friday, Alex and Tom are catching the train. (catch)

2 On Friday, Tom is cooking dinner. (cook)

3 On Saturday, they 're meeting Paul. (meet)

4 On Sunday, Tom isn't making sandwiches. (make)

5 On Sunday, they aren't going skiing. (go)

**7** ★★ **Complete Alex's sentences. Use the affirmative or negative present continuous of the verbs in the box, and the notes in exercise 6.**

borrow ~~buy~~ catch come cook go leave make meet

We're going camping in Cornwall at the weekend. We **aren't buying** a new tent. Tom (**1**) is borrowing his friend Joe's tent.

On Friday we (**2**) 're catching the train. I (**3**) 'm not cooking dinner on Friday night but I (**4**) 'm making sandwiches on Sunday.

We (**5**) 're meeting our friend Paul at the campsite on Saturday.

On Sunday we (**6**) 're going windsurfing. We (**7**) 're not leaving on Sunday night. We (**8**) 're coming home on Monday.

**8** ★★★ **Write true sentences about weekend plans. Use the present continuous and a future time phrase.**

*I'm going out on Saturday night.*

1 I Students' answers ______.

2 My parents ______.

3 My best friend ______.

4 Our teacher ______.

## *must / mustn't*

**9** ★ **Choose the correct options.**

We (**must**) / **mustn't** buy a present. It's her birthday.

1 We **must** / (**mustn't**) miss our plane.

2 He must (**leave**) / **leaves** now!

3 You (**must**) / **mustn't** wear suncream. It's very hot.

4 They **must** / (**mustn't**) use their mobile phones on the plane.

**10** ★★ **Complete the sentences. Use *must* or *mustn't* and the verbs in the box.**

~~be~~ carry listen stand take

AEROPLANE RULES

1 Bags **mustn't be** more than 25 kilograms.

2 Passengers mustn't carry matches on the aeroplane.

3 Passengers must listen to the safety instructions.

4 Passengers mustn't take pets on the aeroplane.

5 Children mustn't stand on their seats.

**11** ★★★ **What are your school rules? Write two affirmative and two negative rules. Use *must* and *mustn't*.**

✓ *Students must arrive at school on time.*

1 ✓ Students' answers ______

2 ✓ ______

3 ✗ ______

4 ✗ ______

# Around the world

**1** ★ **Complete the chart. Use the words in the box.**

~~Antarctica~~ Arctic Asia Caribbean
Central America Indian
Mediterranean Pacific

| Continents | Oceans | Seas |
|---|---|---|
| Antarctica | (3) Artic | (6) Caribbean |
| (1) Asia | (4) Indian | (7) Mediterranean |
| (2) Central America | (5) Pacific | |

**2** ★★ **Complete the words.**

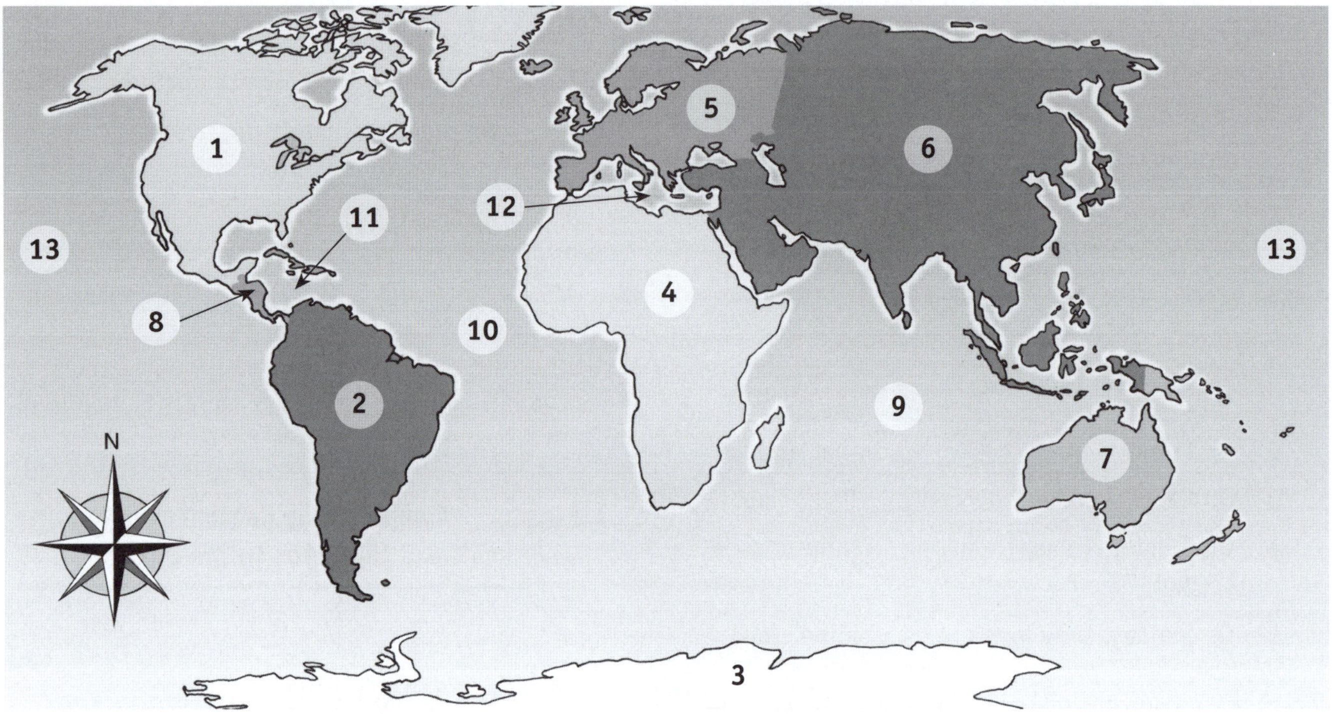


1 North America
2 South America
3 Antarctica
4 Africa
5 Europe
6 Asia
7 Oceania
8 Central America
9 Indian Ocean
10 Atlantic Ocean
11 Caribbean Sea
12 Mediterranean Sea
13 Pacific Ocean

**3** ★★★ **Complete the quiz.**

There are many countries in this continent. They include Japan and India. Asia

1 The countries in this continent include Austria and part of Russia. Europe

2 This continent is south of the Mediterranean Sea and east of the Atlantic Ocean. Africa

3 Nine countries in this continent have got Spanish as their first language. South America

4 This sea is east of Central America and south of North America. Caribbean Sea

5 Snow covers almost all of this cold ocean for ten months every year. Arctic Ocean

6 The islands Madagascar, the Maldives and Sri Lanka are in this ocean. Indian Ocean


Vocabulary Bank pages 100–101

## Holiday films

**1 What do you do to remember your holidays?**

In 2003, American Matt Harding lived in Australia. He made computer games but he was bored. He wanted to travel.

Two months later, Matt was in Hanoi, Vietnam. He made a film for his friends. In the film, he danced in Hanoi. Then he danced in other famous places. Matt danced badly and the film was funny. He put it on the Internet and soon he was famous!

In his first film Matt danced in fifteen countries. He made two more films, in 2006 and in 2008. In his third film he danced in 42 different countries, on seven continents. In 2008, almost fifteen million people watched Matt's third film!

Maybe Matt is going to be dancing near you soon. Go and dance with him!

*A street in Hanoi, the first place Matt danced in.*

**2 ★ Read the text. How many films did Matt make?** 3

**3 ★★ Are these sentences true or false? Write T or F.**

Matt is Australian. F

1 He enjoyed his job. F
2 He first danced in Vietnam. T
3 He dances well. F
4 He made the first film because he wanted to become famous. F
5 In total, he made three films. T
6 He danced in fifteen countries in his third film. F

**4 ★★★ Answer the questions.**

Where is Matt from?
He's from America.

1 Why did Matt leave his job?
He was bored.
2 Why did he make his first film?
He made his first film for his friends.
3 Where did Matt first dance?
Matt first danced in Vietnam.
4 Why was Matt's first film funny?
It was funny because Matt danced badly.
5 When did Matt make his second film?
Matt made his second film in 2006.
6 How many people watched Matt's third film in 2008?
Almost fifteen million people watched Matt's third film in 2008.

## Invitations

**1** ★ **Complete the dialogue. Use the sentences in the box.**

| |
|---|
| ~~Do you want to come with me?~~ |
| Do you want to come with us? I'd love to! |
| I hope they say yes! Sorry, I can't. |
| We're going to watch the Formula One race. |

| | |
|---|---|
| **Carla** | I'm going to the shopping centre on Saturday. *Do you want to come with me?* |
| **Julian** | (1) Sorry, I can't. I'm going to Silverstone with my cousins. (2) We're going to watch the Formula One race. |
| **Carla** | Wow! That sounds like fun! |
| **Julian** | (3) Do you want to come with us? I can ask my aunt and uncle. |
| **Carla** | (4) I'd love to! But I must ask my parents first. |
| **Julian** | OK. (5) I hope they say yes! |

**2** ★★ **Answer the questions.**

Where is Carla going on Saturday?
*She's going to the shopping centre.*

1 Where is Julian going on Saturday?
He's going to Silverstone.

2 Who is he going with?
He's going with his cousins.

3 What is he going to do?
He's going to watch the Formula One race.

4 Who must Carla ask for permission?
She must ask her parents for permission.

**3** ★★★ **In your notebook, write a dialogue like the dialogue in exercise 1. Use the ideas in the box.**

| |
|---|
| library |
| windsurfing in the Lake District with dad |

## Dictation

**4** ★★ 4.10 **Listen. Listen again and write the sentences in your notebook.**



## Sequence markers

**1** ★ **Put the sentences in this dream holiday in the correct order.**

1 Then I'm going to stay for a week in a village in the Alphujarras. 2

2 Finally, I'm going to Barcelona to see a football match. 4

3 After that, I'm going to Madrid to visit the Prado. 3

4 First, I'm going to the Alhambra, in Spain. 1

**2** ★★ **Complete the paragraph. Use the words in the box.**

| |
|---|
| After that Finally ~~First~~ Then |

My dream holiday is in South America. *First*, I'm going to Easter Island in Chile. I want to see the old statues. (1) Then I'm going to Machu Picchu in Peru. The Incas were amazing. (2) After that, I'm going to the Amazon rainforest in Brazil. I want to see the animals there. (3) Finally, I'm going to the Iguazu Falls in Argentina. The waterfall looks fantastic!

**3** ★★★ **Complete Julie's holiday plan. Use her notes and use sequencing words.**

*My dream holiday*

* visit the North Pole
* walk along the Great Wall of China
* climb Mount Everest in the Himalayas
* Go snorkelling in the Great Barrier Reef in Australia

*My dream holiday is a long one! First, I'm going to visit the North Pole. I think it's an amazing place and I love geography.*
(1) Then I'm going to walk *along the Great Wall of China. It's over 6,000 kilometres long!*
(2) After that, I'm going to climb *Mount Everest in the Himalayas.*
(3) Finally, I'm going to go snorkelling *in the Great Barrier Reef in Australia. The perfect end to a perfect holiday!*

 Writing Builder page 110

# Contents


## Welcome 64

*be*: present simple
Possessive *'s*
Demonstrative pronouns

## Unit 1 66

*have got*
Pronouns and possessive adjectives

## Unit 2 68

Present simple affirmative
Adverbs of frequency
*can / can't*

## Unit 3 70

Present simple negative and interrogative
Question words

## Unit 4 72

Present continuous
Present tense contrast
Prepositions of place

## Unit 5 74

*there's / there are*
Imperative

## Unit 6 76

Countable and uncountable nouns
*some* and *any*
Indefinite pronouns

## Unit 7 78

*be*: past simple
*there was / there were*

## Unit 8 80

Past simple affirmative (regular verbs)
Past simple affirmative (irregular verbs)
Adverbs of manner

## Unit 9 82

*going to*
Present continuous with future meaning
*must / mustn't*

## *be*: present simple

| Afirmativa | Formas contractas |
|---|---|
| I am | I'm |
| you are | you're |
| he is | he's |
| she is | she's |
| it is | it's |
| we are | we're |
| you are | you're |
| they are | they're |

Al hablar se suelen utilizar las formas contractas.

| Negativa | Formas contractas |
|---|---|
| I am not | I'm not |
| you are not | you aren't |
| he is not | he isn't |
| she is not | she isn't |
| it is not | it isn't |
| we are not | we aren't |
| you are not | you aren't |
| they are not | they aren't |

La negativa se forma colocando *not* detrás de *am*, *are*, *is*. Las formas contractas (*'m not*, *isn't*, *aren't*) son más frecuentes.

I'm not French. No soy francés.

| Interrogativa | Respuestas breves | |
|---|---|---|
| | Afirmativa | Negativa |
| Am I ...? | Yes, I am. | No, I'm not. |
| Are you ...? | Yes, you are. | No, you aren't. |
| Is he ...? | Yes, he is. | No, he isn't. |
| Is she ...? | Yes, she is. | No, she isn't. |
| Is it ...? | Yes, it is. | No, it isn't. |
| Are we ...? | Yes, we are. | No, we aren't. |
| Are you ...? | Yes, you are. | No, you aren't. |
| Are they ...? | Yes, they are. | No, they aren't. |

La interrogativa se forma colocando *Am*, *Are*, *Is* delante del sujeto. La interrogación va al final de la frase.

Are you from Paris? ¿Eres de París?

En las respuestas breves de la forma negativa se suelen utilizar las formas contractas (*'m not*, *aren't*, *isn't*).

'Are you Canadian?' 'No, we aren't.' "¿Sois canadienses?" "No."

### Usos

El verbo *be* se traduce por "ser", "estar" y "tener" (con edades).

My friends are from Greece. Mis amigos son de Greece.
Cambridge is in England. Cambridge está en Inglaterra.
Paul is fifteen years old. Paul tiene quince años.

**! ¡Ojo!**

Con ciertas expresiones se utiliza *be*, y no *have*.

I'm fourteen. (NO ~~I have fourteen.~~)
I'm thirsty. (NO ~~I have thirsty.~~)
I'm cold. (NO ~~I have cold.~~)

## Possessive *'s*

**Posesivo en *'s***

Se añade *'s* a sustantivos y nombres propios para expresar posesión.

Jane's dad (NO ~~the dad of Jane~~) el padre de Jane
my sister's friend (NO ~~the friend of my sister~~) la amiga / el amigo de mi hermana

Con sustantivos en plural acabados en *s*, sólo se añade el apóstrofo (').

his friends' class la clase de sus amigos

Con nombres de lugares y cosas se utiliza la preposición *of*, y no la forma *'s*.

The capital of Spain is Madrid. (NO ~~Spain's capital is Madrid.~~) La capital de España es Madrid.
the title of the book (NO ~~the book's title~~) el título del libro

## Demonstrative pronouns

**Pronombres demostrativos**

| Singular | Plural |
|---|---|
| this (este / esta / esto) | these (estos / estas) |
| that (ese / esa / eso, aquel / aquella / aquello) | those (esos / esas, aquellos / aquellas) |

En inglés, los pronombres demostrativos sólo tienen singular y plural. No muestran variación de género.

*This* y *these* se refieren a algo o alguien que está cercano a la persona que habla.

This is a pencil. Esto es un lápiz.
These are my books. Estos son mis libros.

*That* y *those* se refieren a personas y cosas que están más lejos de la persona que habla.

That's my brother. Ese / Aquel es mi hermano.
Those are his French books. Esos / Aquellos son sus libros de francés.

*This* se utiliza para presentar a la gente.

This is Joseph. Este es Joseph.

*That* se utiliza para confirmar que algo es correcto.

'Are you Mary?' 'That's right.' (NO ~~'Yes.'~~) "¿Eres Mary?" "Sí."

## *be*: present simple

**1 Complete the sentences. Use the affirmative of *be*.**

I'm fourteen.

1 I 'm ______ in that class.
2 We 're ______ from Seville.
3 You 're ______ a student.
4 My pen 's ______ blue.
5 My mum and dad are ______ at the cinema.

**2 Make the sentences in exercise 1 negative.**

I'm not fourteen.

1 I 'm not ______ in that class.
2 We aren't ______ from Seville.
3 You aren't ______ a student.
4 My pen isn't ______ blue.
5 My mum and dad aren't ______ at the cinema.

**3 Complete the questions. Then write short true answers.**

Is Beyoncé from France?
No, she isn't.

1 Are ______ Jay-Z and Madonna singers?
Yes, they are.
2 Are ______ you twelve?
Students' answers
3 Is ______ Oxford in Italy?
No, it isn't.
4 Are ______ you and your friends in class?
Students' answers

## Possessive *'s*

**4 Rewrite the sentences. Use the possessive *'s* and *'*.**

Tom has got a car. It's big.
Tom's car is big.

1 My sister has got a bike. It's new.
My sister's bike is new.
2 My parents have got a house. It's small.
My parents' house is small.
3 Andrew has got a sister. She's eleven.
Andrew's sister is eleven.

**5 Rewrite the phrases. Use the possessive *'s*, the possessive *'* and *of*.**

my brothers / computer
my brothers' computer
the basketball team / the name
the name of the basketball team

1 England / the capital
the capital of England
2 the teacher / book
the teacher's book
3 your friend / pet
your friend's pet
4 the film / the end
the end of the film
5 her eyes / the colour
the colour of her eyes
6 the students / classroom
the students' classroom

## Demonstrative pronouns

**6 Complete the sentences. Use *this* or *these*.**

This is my dog.

1 These ______ aren't my books.
2 Is this ______ your brother?
3 These ______ are your parents.
4 Are these ______ our desks?
5 This ______ is a green pencil.

**7 Complete the sentences. Use *that* or *those*.**

Those are my pens.

1 That ______'s my teacher.
2 That ______ isn't my classroom.
3 Are those ______ your grandparents?
4 That ______'s our CD player.
5 Are those ______ your books?

## *have got*

| Afirmativa | Formas contractas |
|---|---|
| I have got | I've got |
| you have got | you've got |
| he has got | he's got |
| she has got | she's got |
| it has got | it's got |
| we have got | we've got |
| you have got | you've got |
| they have got | they've got |

En la tercera persona del singular, *have got* se convierte en *has got*.

Mary has got long hair. Mary tiene el pelo largo.

Al hablar se suelen utilizar las formas contractas.

You've got fair hair. Tienes el pelo rubio.

| Negativa | Formas contractas |
|---|---|
| I have not got | I haven't got |
| you have not got | you haven't got |
| he has not got | he hasn't got |
| she has not got | she hasn't got |
| it has not got | it hasn't got |
| we have not got | we haven't got |
| you have not got | you haven't got |
| they have not got | they haven't got |

La negativa se forma colocando *not* detrás de *have* y *has*. Las formas contractas (*haven't got*, *hasn't got*) son más frecuentes.

Jim hasn't got a brother. Jim no tiene un hermano.

| Interrogativa | Respuestas breves | |
|---|---|---|
| | Afirmativa | Negativa |
| Have I got …? | Yes, I have. | No, I haven't. |
| Have you got …? | Yes, you have. | No, you haven't. |
| Has he got …? | Yes, he has. | No, he hasn't. |
| Has she got …? | Yes, she has. | No, she hasn't. |
| Has it got …? | Yes, it has. | No, it hasn't. |
| Have we got …? | Yes, we have. | No, we haven't. |
| Have you got …? | Yes, you have. | No, you haven't. |
| Have they got …? | Yes, they have. | No, they haven't. |

La interrogativa se forma colocando *Have*, *Has* delante del sujeto. La interrogación va al final de la frase.

Has David got a car? ¿David tiene un coche?

En las respuestas breves no se utiliza *got*.

'Have you got a pencil?' 'Yes, I have.' (NO ~~Yes, I have got.~~)

### Usos

*Have got* se utiliza para expresar posesión. Significa "tener".

I've got a computer. Tengo un ordenador.
I haven't got a sister. No tengo una hermana.
'Have you got a cat?' 'Yes, I have.' "¿Tienes gato?" "Sí."

*Have got* se utiliza para describir el aspecto físico de las personas.

He's got green eyes. Tiene los ojos verdes.
She hasn't got short hair. No tiene el pelo corto.
'Has he got blue eyes?' 'No, he hasn't.' "¿Tiene los ojos azules?" "No."

**! ¡Ojo!**

En la forma interrogativa de *have got* no se utiliza *Do / Does*.

Have you got a ruler? (NO ~~Do you have got a ruler?~~)

## Pronouns and possessive adjectives

**Pronombres y adjetivos posesivos**

| Pronombre sujeto | Adjetivo posesivo |
|---|---|
| I | my (mi, mis) |
| you | your (tu, tus, su, sus –de usted–) |
| he | his (su, sus –de él–) |
| she | her (su, sus –de ella–) |
| it | its (su, sus –de un objeto o animal–) |
| we | our (nuestro / a, nuestros / as) |
| you | your (vuestro / a, vuestros / as, su, sus –de ustedes–) |
| they | their (su, sus –de ellos / as–) |

Los adjetivos posesivos acompañan a los sustantivos.

We like our teacher. Nos gusta nuestra profesora.
Where's my pen? ¿Dónde está mi bolígrafo?

Hay tres adjetivos posesivos de 3ª persona del singular: *his*, *her*, *its*.

Mark likes his mobile phone. A Mark le gusta su teléfono móvil -la de él-.
Ann likes her new T-shirt. A Ann le gusta su camiseta nueva -la de ella-.
The cat likes its food. Al gato le gusta su comida -la de un animal-.

Hay un solo adjetivo posesivo de 3ª persona del plural: *their*.

They like their classroom. Les gusta su clase -la de ellos / ellas-.

Los adjetivos posesivos no tienen variación de número. No cambian dependiendo de si se posee una cosa o varias.

my hair / my eyes mi pelo / mis ojos
your nose / your glasses tu nariz / tus gafas
his brother / his parents su hermano / sus padres
its food / its toys su comida / sus juguetes
our dog / our books nuestra perro / nuestros libros
your house / your friends vuestra casa / vuestros amigos
their sister / their grandparents su hermana / sus abuelos

**! ¡Ojo!**

Ten cuidado al utilizar *its* e *it's*.

*its* = adjetivo posesivo

My cat is brown, but its eyes are green.

*it's* = *it is* ("es")

'What's this?' 'It's a pencil.'

## have got

**1 Write affirmative, negative and interrogative sentences. Use *have got*.**

Marco / a brother
Marco has got a brother.
Marco hasn't got a brother.
Has Marco got a brother?

1 your cousins / a beautiful house
Your cousins have got a beautiful house.
Your cousins haven't got a beautiful house.
Have your cousins got a beautiful house?

2 he / a green T-shirt
He's got a green T-shirt.
He hasn't got a green T-shirt.
Has he got a green T-shirt?

3 they / a small classroom
They've got a small classroom.
They haven't got a small classroom.
Have they got a small classroom?

4 your teacher / a dictionary
Your teacher's got a dictionary.
Your teacher hasn't got a dictionary.
Has your teacher got a dictionary?

5 she / short hair
She's got short hair.
She hasn't got short hair.
Has she got short hair?

**2 Write affirmative and negative sentences. Use *have got*.**

| | Carmen | Luis and Ana |
|---|---|---|
| a bike | ✓ | (3) ✗ |
| a cat | (1) ✗ | (4) ✓ |
| an MP3 player | (2) ✓ | (5) ✓ |

Carmen has got a bike.
1 Carmen hasn't got a cat.
2 Carmen has got an MP3 player.
3 Luis and Ana haven't got a bike.
4 Luis and Ana have got a cat.
5 Luis and Ana have got an MP3 player.

**3 Make the sentences in exercise 2 questions. Then write short answers.**

Has Carmen got a bike? Yes, she has.
1 Has Carmen got a cat?
No, she hasn't.
2 Has Carmen got an MP3 player?
Yes, she has.
3 Have Luis and Ana got a bike?
No, they haven't.
4 Have Luis and Ana got a cat?
Yes, they have.
5 Have Luis and Ana got an MP3 player?
Yes, they have.

**4 Complete the dialogue. Use the correct forms of *have got*.**

**Eve** Have you got a brother or a sister?
**Sue** I **(1)** haven't got a sister but I **(2)** 've got a brother. He's sixteen. His name's John and he **(3)** 's got short hair.
**Eve** **(4)** Has he got blue eyes or brown eyes?
**Sue** He **(5)** hasn't got blue eyes or brown eyes. He **(6)** 's got green eyes.
**Eve** **(7)** Has he got a girlfriend?
**Sue** No, he **(8)** hasn't.

## Pronouns and possessive adjectives

**5 Complete the sentences. Use the correct possessive adjectives.**

I do my homework.
1 You do your homework.
2 She does her homework.
3 He does his homework.
4 We do our homework.
5 They do their homework.

## Present simple affirmative

***Present simple*** **afirmativa**

| Afirmativa | | |
|---|---|---|
| I play | you play | |
| he plays | she plays | it plays |
| we play | you play | they play |

A excepción de la 3ª persona del singular (*he / she / it*), la forma afirmativa coincide con la del infinitivo sin *to* del verbo.

### Spelling rules: 3rd person singular

**Reglas ortográficas: 3ª persona del singular**

1 La forma de la 3ª persona del singular (*he / she / it*) siempre termina en *-s*.
She reads magazines. My dog likes hamburgers. He plays the piano.

2 Los verbos que terminan en consonante + *-y* cambian la *-y* por *-ies*.
She studies German.
Si el verbo termina en vocal + *-y*, sólo se añade *-s*.
play / plays buy / buys

3 Si el verbo termina en *-ss*, *-ch*, *-sh*, *-x*, *-o*, se añade *-es*.
He watches music videos. She finishes school at three.
This train goes to Oxford.

4 El verbo *have* es un verbo irregular, y tiene una forma especial (*has*).
I have got red hair.
She has got three brothers.

### Usos

1 Explicar cosas que suceden habitualmente y describir rutinas de todos los días, todas las semanas, etc.
I listen to music every day. Escucho música todos los días.
She goes to the cinema on Saturday. Va al cine el sábado.

2 Expresar verdades generales y definiciones.
La Feria de Abril is a Spanish festival. La Feria de Abril es una fiesta española.
Liverpool is a city in England. Liverpool es una ciudad de Inglaterra.

3 Indicar gustos, opiniones y sentimientos.
I like Brad Pitt. Me gusta Brad Pitt.
Dylan thinks English is difficult. Dylan cree que el inglés es difícil.

Consulta en la página 70 las formas interrogativa y negativa del *present simple*.

## Adverbs of frequency

**Adverbios de frecuencia**

0% never almost never sometimes often usually always 100%

Los adverbios de frecuencia se suelen colocar delante del verbo.

They never watch TV in the morning. Nunca ven la tele por la mañana.

En el caso del verbo *be*, se colocan detrás.

He's never late. Nunca llega tarde.

## *can / can't*

La forma *can* es la misma para todas las personas del verbo. La afirmativa se forma colocando *can* delante del infinitivo del verbo principal.

*I can, you can, he / she / it can, we can, you can, they can go.*

I can speak English. Sé hablar inglés.

I can go to the park. Puedo ir al parque.

La negativa se forma colocando *not* detrás de *can* (*cannot*). Es la misma para todas las personas del verbo. La forma contracta *can't* es más frecuente.

*I can't, you can't, he / she / it can't, we can't, you can't, they can't go.*

I can't go to the cinema on Friday. No puedo ir al cine el viernes.

I can't play tennis. No sé jugar al tenis.

La interrogativa se forma colocando *can* al principio de la frase, delante del sujeto.

*Can I, you, he / she / it, we, you, they go?*

En las respuestas breves, el verbo principal se omite y se utilizan sólo *can / can't* para la afirmativa y negativa.

'Can you play the guitar?' 'Yes, I can.' / 'No, I can't.' "¿Sabes tocar la guitarra?" "Sí."/ "No."

### Usos

1 *Can* expresa habilidad o capacidad para hacer algo. Se traduce por "poder" o "saber".
I can speak French. Sé hablar francés.
I can swim. Sé nadar.
I can't open the window. No puedo abrir la ventana.

2 *Can* sirve para pedir y dar permiso.
'Can I go to the park?' 'Yes, you can.' "¿Puedo ir al parque?" "Sí."

## Present simple affirmative

**1 Complete the sentences. Use the verbs in the box.**

go listen ~~play~~ read start

He plays computer games in the evening.

1 They go to the cinema.
2 She reads magazines.
3 The TV programme starts at seven o'clock.
4 I listen to pop music.

**2 Write the third person singular forms.**

study studies
1 watch watches
2 play plays
3 chat chats
4 teach teaches
5 go goes
6 meet meets
7 do does
8 carry carries

## Adverbs of frequency

**3 Put the words in the correct order to write sentences.**

in the park. / usually / She / friends / meets
She usually meets friends in the park.

1 always / David / happy / is / on Saturday mornings.
David is always happy on Saturday mornings.
2 plays / tennis. / never / My sister
My sister never plays tennis.
3 Sarah / does / often / in the afternoon. / puzzles
Sarah often does puzzles in the afternoon.
4 to the cinema. / My dad / almost never / goes
My dad almost never goes to the cinema.
5 great. / are / Comics / usually
Comics are usually great.

**4 Add adverbs of frequency to make the sentences true for you.**

I watch DVDs at home.
I sometimes watch DVDs at home.

1 I chat with my friends in class.
Students' answers
2 I go to the cinema on Sunday.
3 I am early for school.
4 I play basketball.
5 I am nice to my family.
6 I speak English in my English lessons.
7 I have a shower in the evening.
8 I do my homework.

## *can / can't*

**5 Correct the mistakes in the sentences.**

I can plays hockey.
I can play hockey.

1 'Can you speak English?' 'Yes, can.'
'Can you speak English?' 'Yes, I can.'
2 He go cans to the park.
He can go to the park.
3 We can't to see a film.
We can't see a film.
4 'They can meet at six o'clock?' 'No, they can't.'
'Can they meet at six o'clock?' 'No, they can't.'
5 I no can play football.
I can't play football.
6 She can plays computer games.
She can play computer games.

# Present simple negative and interrogative

***Present simple*** **negativa e interrogativa**

| Negativa | Formas contractas |
|---|---|
| I do not teach | I don't teach |
| you do not teach | you don't teach |
| he does not teach<br>she does not teach<br>it does not teach | he doesn't teach<br>she doesn't teach<br>it doesn't teach |
| we do not teach<br>you do not teach<br>they do not teach | we don't teach<br>you don't teach<br>they don't teach |

La negativa se forma colocando *do not* / *does not* delante del infinitivo sin *to* del verbo principal.

We don't speak Italian. No hablamos italiano.

| Interrogativa | Respuestas breves | |
|---|---|---|
| | Afirmativa | Negativa |
| Do I teach? | Yes, I do. | No, I don't. |
| Do you teach? | Yes, you do. | No, you don't. |
| Does he teach?<br>Does she teach?<br>Does it teach? | Yes, he does.<br>Yes, she does.<br>Yes, it does. | No, he doesn't.<br>No, she doesn't.<br>No, it doesn't. |
| Do we teach?<br>Do you teach?<br>Do they teach? | Yes, we do.<br>Yes, you do.<br>Yes, they do. | No, we don't.<br>No, you don't.<br>No, they don't. |

La interrogativa se forma colocando *Do*, *Does* delante del sujeto.

Does she like Real Madrid? ¿Le gusta el Real Madrid?

En las respuestas breves se omite el verbo principal (*play*, *teach*, etc.) y se utiliza únicamente el auxiliar *do* / *does*.

'Do they go swimming?' 'Yes, they do.' "¿Suelen ir a nadar?" "Sí."

En la forma negativa de las respuestas breves se suelen utilizar las formas contractas (*don't*, *doesn't*).

'Do you study German?' 'No, I don't.' "¿Estudias alemán?" "No."

**! ¡Ojo!**

El verbo principal no lleva *s* en la 3ª persona del singular de las formas negativa e interrogativa.

She doesn't live in London. (NO ~~She doesn't lives in London.~~)

Does he play basketball? (NO ~~Does he plays basketball?~~)

Consulta en la página 68 los usos del *present simple*.

# Question words

**Partículas interrogativas**

**Who ¿Quién?**

Who is your favourite singer? ¿Quién es tu cantante preferido?

**When ¿Cuándo? / ¿A qué hora?**

When is your birthday? ¿Cuándo es tu cumpleaños?

When do you go to bed? ¿A qué hora te sueles acostar?

**How often ¿Con qué frecuencia?**

How often do you play tennis? ¿Con qué frecuencia juegas al tenis?

**What ¿Qué / ¿Cuál?**

What programmes do you watch on TV? ¿Qué programas ves en la tele?

What's your favourite subject? ¿Cuál es tu asignatura preferida?

What sports do you like? ¿Qué deportes te gustan?

**How ¿Cómo?**

'How are you?' 'Fine, thanks.' "¿Cómo / Qué tal estás?" "Bien, gracias."

How do you spell 'science'? ¿Cómo se deletrea "*science*"?

**Where ¿Dónde?**

Where is my dictionary? ¿Dónde está mi diccionario?

Where do you live? ¿Dónde vives?

**Why ¿Por qué?**

'Why do you like him?' 'Because he's fun.'

"¿Por qué te gusta?" "Porque es divertido."

**Which ¿Qué / Cuál?**

Se utiliza cuando hay un número de personas o cosas limitado.

Which actor do you prefer, Brad Pitt or George Clooney? ¿Qué actor prefieres, Brad Pitt o George Clooney?

Which bus do you take to school? ¿Qué autobús coges para ir al colegio?

# Present simple negative and interrogative

**1 Put the words in the correct order to make sentences.**

to school. / She / take / doesn't / the bus
She doesn't take the bus to school.

1 don't / timetable. / I / like / my
I don't like my timetable.

2 Bristol. / doesn't / Rafa / in / live
Rafa doesn't live in Bristol.

3 They / study / French. / don't
They don't study French.

4 Italian. / doesn't / She / speak
She doesn't speak Italian.

**2 Complete the sentences. Use *don't* or *doesn't* and the verbs in the box.**

~~like~~ play sit walk work

I like basketball but I don't like volleyball.

1 George watches tennis on TV but he doesn't play it.

2 My aunt lives in Madrid but she doesn't work there.

3 Alice goes to school by bike. She doesn't walk .

4 My cousin is in my class but I don't sit next to her.

**3 Make the sentences negative.**

Ted and Peter usually have lunch at school.
Ted and Peter don't usually have lunch at school.

1 Sam goes swimming.
Sam doesn't go swimming.

2 I go to the shopping centre on Saturday.
I don't go to the shopping centre on Saturday.

3 We go cycling at the weekend.
We don't go cycling at the weekend.

4 You play basketball with Victor.
You don't play basketball with Victor.

**4 Write questions and short answers.**

| On Sunday | Jason | Tony and Diana |
|---|---|---|
| listen to music | ✗ | ✓ |
| go to the park | (1) ✗ | (3) ✓ |
| play basketball | (2) ✓ | (4) ✗ |

Does Jason listen to music on Sunday?
No, he doesn't.
Do Tony and Diana listen to music on Sunday?
Yes, they do.

1 Does Jason go to the park on Sunday?
No, he doesn't.

2 Does Jason play basketball on Sunday?
Yes, he does.

3 Do Tony and Diana go to the park on Sunday?
Yes, they do.

4 Do Tony and Diana play basketball on Sunday?
No, they don't.

# Question words

**5 Complete the questions. Use the words in the box.**

how ~~what~~ when where who why

1 What's his name?
2 Why do you like art?
3 How often do you go to the cinema?
4 Where do you live?
5 When do you have lunch?
6 Who 's your favourite actress?

**6 Match the questions in exercise 5 with the correct answers.**

Paul Williams. 1

a) Every weekend. 3
b) Penélope Cruz. 6
c) At half past twelve. 5
d) In Oxford. 4
e) Because it's interesting. 2

## Present continuous

***Present continuous***

| Afirmativa | Formas contractas |
|---|---|
| I am playing | I'm playing |
| you are playing | you're playing |
| he is playing<br>she is playing<br>it is playing | he's playing<br>she's playing<br>it's playing |
| we are playing<br>you are playing<br>they are playing | we're playing<br>you're playing<br>they're playing |

El *present continuous*, se forma con el *present simple* del auxiliar *be* y la forma en *-ing* del verbo principal.

We're visiting Valencia. Estamos de visita en Valencia.

| Negativa | Formas contractas |
|---|---|
| I am not playing | I'm not playing |
| you are not playing | you aren't playing |
| he is not playing<br>she is not playing<br>it is not playing | he isn't playing<br>she isn't playing<br>it isn't playing |
| we are not playing<br>you are not playing<br>they are not playing | we aren't playing<br>you aren't playing<br>they aren't playing |

La negativa se forma colocando *not* detrás del verbo *be*. Las formas contractas son más frecuentes.

It isn't raining. No está lloviendo.

| Interrogativa | Respuestas breves | |
|---|---|---|
| | Afirmativa | Negativa |
| Am I playing? | Yes, I am. | No, I'm not. |
| Are you playing? | Yes, you are. | No, you aren't. |
| Is he playing?<br>Is she playing?<br>Is it playing? | Yes, he is.<br>Yes, she is.<br>Yes, it is. | No, he isn't.<br>No, she isn't.<br>No, it isn't. |
| Are we playing?<br>Are you playing?<br>Are they playing? | Yes, we are.<br>Yes, you are.<br>Yes, they are. | No, we aren't.<br>No, you aren't.<br>No, they aren't. |

La interrogativa se forma colocando *Am, Are, Is* delante del sujeto.

Are they doing aerobics? ¿Están haciendo aerobic?

En las respuestas breves se omite el verbo principal (*playing*, *eating*, etc.) y se utiliza únicamente el auxiliar *be*.

'Are you cooking?' 'Yes, I am.' "¿Estás cocinando?" "Sí."

En la forma negativa de las respuestas breves se suelen utilizar las formas contractas (*'m not, aren't, isn't*).

'Is he playing tennis?' 'No, he isn't.' "¿Está jugando al tenis?" "No."

### Spelling rules: *-ing* form

**Reglas ortográficas: forma en *-ing* del verbo**

1 Con la mayoría de los verbos, se añade *-ing* al infinitivo sin *to*.
play / playing speak / speaking sing / singing

2 Con verbos acabados en *-e*, la *-e* se pierde y se añade *-ing*.
write / writing dance / dancing phone / phoning

3 Con verbos acabados en una consonante precedida de una sola vocal, la consonante se duplica y se añade *-ing*.
run / running chat / chatting get / getting

### Usos

El *present continuous* se utiliza para describir acciones que están sucediendo mientras se habla. A menudo va acompañado de expresiones como *now* (ahora), *at the moment* (en este momento) y *today* (hoy).

We're having a lot of fun today. Hoy nos estamos divirtiendo mucho.
I'm doing my homework at the moment. En este momento estoy haciendo los deberes.

**! ¡Ojo!**

Los verbos que expresan sentimientos y procesos mentales no se suelen utilizar en la forma continua. Son verbos como *understand* (entender), *think* (pensar), *know* (saber), *like* (gustar), *love* (amar), *hate* (odiar) y *want* (querer).

I like Shakira. (NO ~~I'm liking Shakira.~~)
I don't know. (NO ~~I'm not knowing.~~)
What do you want? (NO ~~What are you wanting?~~)

Consulta en la página 82 el *present continuous* con valor de futuro.

## Present tense contrast

***Present simple* y *present continuous***

El *present simple* se utiliza para hablar de actividades que se realizan habitualmente o de rutinas. Puede ir acompañado de expresiones de frecuencia como *usually* (normalmente), *often* (a menudo), *in the morning* (por la mañana), etc.

I usually have lunch at school. Normalmente como en el colegio.

El *present continuous* indica actividades que se están realizando en el momento en que se habla. Puede ir acompañado de expresiones como *now* (ahora), *at the moment* (en este momento) y *today* (hoy).

I am having lunch now. Ahora estoy comiendo.

## Prepositions of place

Las preposiciones de lugar se utilizan para expresar dónde se encuentra una persona o cosa.

*behind* = detrás (de)

The bike is behind the tree. La bici está detrás del árbol.

*in* = en (dentro de)

The book is in my bag. El libro está en mi bolsa.

*in front of* = delante de

Carlos is sitting in front of Verónica. Carlos está sentado delante de Verónica.

*next to* = al lado de

The park is next to my school. El parque está al lado de mi colegio.

*on* = en, sobre, encima de

The computer is on the table. El ordenador está encima de la mesa.

*under* = debajo de

The shoes are under the bed. Los zapatos están debajo de la cama.

## Present continuous

**1 Complete the sentences. Use the present continuous affirmative.**

I'm *reading* (read) a magazine.

1 She *'s singing* (sing) a Shakira song.
2 We *'re listening* (listen) to the teacher.
3 I *'m studying* (study).
4 'What's Janet doing?' 'She *'s watching* (watch) TV.'
5 I *'m eating* (eat) a banana.

**2 Write the *-ing* forms of these verbs.**

swim *swimming*
1 chat *chatting*
2 have *having*
3 stop *stopping*
4 study *studying*
5 start *starting*
6 run *running*
7 write *writing*

**3 Make the sentences negative.**

She's drawing a picture.
*She isn't drawing a picture.*

1 We're having breakfast.
*We aren't having breakfast.*
2 It's snowing.
*It isn't snowing.*
3 They're chatting on the Internet.
*They aren't chatting on the Internet.*
4 I'm reading a comic.
*I'm not reading a comic.*

**4 Complete the questions and short answers. Use the correct forms of *be*.**

'*Is* it raining?' 'No, it *isn't*.'

1 '*Are* they having lunch?' 'Yes, they *are*.'
2 '*Is* he studying?' 'Yes, he *is*.'
3 '*Are* you watching TV?' 'No, I *'m not*.'
4 '*Are* we going to Cambridge?' 'No, we *aren't*.'

**5 Write questions and short answers. Use the present continuous.**

Veronica / read? ✗
*Is Veronica reading? No, she isn't.*

1 Daniel / talk / on the phone? ✗
*Is Daniel talking on the phone? No, he isn't.*
2 they / play / the guitar? ✓
*Are they playing the guitar? Yes, they are.*
3 you / prepare / dinner? ✗
*Are you preparing dinner? No, you're not.*
4 it / rain? ✓
*Is it raining? Yes, it is.*

**6 Complete the sentences. Use the present continuous or the present simple.**

Paul *loves* (love) pasta.

1 I *don't understand* (not understand) this exercise.
2 Look! It *'s snowing* (snow).
3 *Do* you *know* (know) my brother?
4 Listen. They *'re speaking* (speak) French.
5 *Does* he *like* (like) Christina?

## Present tense contrast

**7 Choose the correct options.**

Martin **reads** / **is reading** a magazine now. *(is reading)*

1 Look! It **rains** / **'s raining**! *('s raining)*
2 David always **is watching** / **watches** a DVD on Saturday night. *(watches)*
3 I usually **am sending** / **send** emails to Bob. *(send)*
4 Julia **is talking** / **talks** on the phone at the moment. *(is talking)*

## Prepositions of place

**8 Choose the correct options.**

I'm sitting **on** / **under** the chair. *(on)*

1 The book is **in** / **next to** the ruler. *(next to)*
2 The tree is **on** / **behind** the house. *(behind)*
3 The car is **in front of** / **in** the bus. *(in front of)*

## *there's / there are*

| | Afirmativa | Negativa y respuestas breves | Interrogativa |
|---|---|---|---|
| Singular | there is<br>Contracción: there's | there is not<br>Contracción: there isn't | Is there …?<br>Yes, there is. / No, there isn't. |
| Plural | there are | there are not<br>Contracción: there aren't | |

En castellano, una sola palabra (hay) expresa tanto el singular como el plural del verbo "haber"; en inglés, por el contrario, hay una forma para el singular (*there is, there's*) y otra para el plural (*there are*).

En afirmativa y negativa se suelen utilizar las formas contractas (*there's, there isn't, there aren't*).

También se utilizan las formas contractas (*there isn't, there aren't*) en las respuestas breves negativas.

'Is there a computer in the classroom?' 'No, there isn't.' "¿Hay un ordenador en esta clase?" "No."

*There's, There isn't, Is there* se utilizan con sustantivos en singular.

There's a pen on the table. Hay un boli encima de la mesa.
There isn't a car in the garage. No hay ningún coche en el garaje.

Is there a garden in your house? ¿Hay un jardín en tu casa?

*There are, There aren't, Are there* se utilizan con sustantivos en plural.

There are two armchairs in the living room. Hay dos sillones en el salón.
There aren't any chairs in the bedroom. No hay ninguna silla en el dormitorio.
Are there any books on the shelf? ¿Hay algún libro en la estantería?

**! ¡Ojo!**

En las formas negativa e interrogativa se utiliza *any* con los sustantivos que están en plural.

There aren't any CDs in my bag.
Are there any flowers in the garden?

## Imperative

**Imperativo**

La afirmativa se forma con el infinitivo del verbo sin *to*. No lleva sujeto y tiene una única forma para el singular y para el plural (tú, vosotros / as, usted, ustedes). Expresa una orden.

Stand up. Levántate. / Levantaos. / Levántese. / Levántense.
Open the door. Abre la puerta. / Abrid la puerta. / Abra la puerta. / Abran la puerta.

La negativa se forma colocando *Don't* delante del verbo. Expresa prohibición.

Don't use your mobile phone in class! ¡No uséis vuestro teléfono móvil en clase!

Don't drink my water! ¡No te bebas mi agua!

En el imperativo, el verbo *be* también utiliza *Don't*.

Don't be late! ¡No lleguéis tarde!

## Usos

El imperativo se utiliza para dar órdenes e instrucciones.

Se puede añadir la palabra *please* (por favor) para suavizar la orden.

Sit down, please. Siéntate, por favor.
Please repeat after me. Por favor, repetid conmigo.

Cuando se quiere pedir algo con educación no se debe utilizar el imperativo. La fórmula adecuada es *Can you …?*

Can you open the door, please? (NO ~~Open the door!~~) ¿Puedes abrir la puerta, por favor?

## *there's / there are*

**1 Complete the sentences. Use *there's* or *there are*.**

There's a sofa in the living room.

1 There are ______ three bedrooms in our house.
2 There's ______ a clock on the wall.
3 There are ______ lots of big cinemas in Madrid.
4 There are ______ clothes on the bed.

**2 Complete the sentences. Use *there isn't* or *there aren't*.**

There isn't a supermarket next to our school.

1 There aren't ______ any chairs in the kitchen.
2 There isn't ______ a big wardrobe in the bedroom.
3 There aren't ______ any bedrooms on the ground floor.
4 There isn't ______ an enormous garden at our house.

**3 Complete the paragraph. Use the affirmative or negative of *there's* or *there are*.**

There are twenty desks in the classroom and (**1**) there are ______ twenty chairs. (**2**) There's ______ one teacher's desk and (**3**) there's ______ a whiteboard. (**4**) There aren't ______ any pens on the teacher's desk, but (**5**) there are ______ three books. (**6**) There are ______ two shelves on the wall. (**7**) There isn't ______ a CD player, but our teacher has got a cassette player.

**4 Write questions and short answers.**

any pencils on the table? ✓
Are there any pencils on the table?
Yes, there are.

1 a mirror in the bathroom? ✗
Is there a mirror in the bathroom?
No, there isn't.

2 any boxes on the shelf? ✗
Are there any boxes on the shelf?
No, there aren't.

3 a TV in your bedroom? ✓
Is there a TV in your bedroom?
Yes, there is.

4 any photos on the wall? ✓
Are there any photos on the wall?
Yes, there are.

## Imperative

**5 Make the affirmative orders negative. Make the negative orders affirmative.**

Don't sit down! Stand up!
Sit down! Don't stand up!

1 Don't play computer games! Read a book!
Play computer games! Don't read a book!

2 Don't close the door! Open it!
Close the door! Don't open it!

3 Don't talk in class! Listen to your teacher!
Talk in class! Don't listen to your teacher!

4 Don't turn on the TV! Turn it off!
Turn on the TV! Don't turn it off!

5 Don't be late! Be early!
Be late! Don't be early!

6 Don't sit in the kitchen! Sit in the living room!
Sit in the kitchen! Don't sit in the living room!

**6 Add *please* to each imperative sentence.**

Don't touch that!
Don't touch that, please.
**or**
Please don't touch that.

1 Eat your breakfast!
Eat your breakfast, please. / Please eat your breakfast.

2 Don't write on the book!
Don't write on the book, please. / Please don't write on the book.

3 Be early!
Be early, please. / Please be early.

4 Don't turn on the computer!
Don't turn on the computer, please. / Please don't turn on the computer.

5 Do your homework!
Do your homework, please. / Please do your homework.

6 Get up!
Get up, please. / Please get up.

## Countable and uncountable nouns

**Sustantivos contables e incontables**

Los sustantivos contables tienen formas de singular y plural. El verbo de la frase concuerda con ellos en número.

banana / bananas
egg / eggs
The banana is in the fridge. El plátano está en el frigorífico.
The eggs are for lunch. Los huevos son para la hora de comer.

Delante de los sustantivos contables se utiliza el artículo indefinido *a* / *an* o un número.

an orange una naranja
two biscuits dos galletas

Los sustantivos incontables no tienen forma de plural. El verbo de la frase siempre va en singular.

This milk is delicious. (NO ~~The milks are delicious.~~) Esta leche está deliciosa.

Los sustantivos incontables no pueden ir acompañados del artículo indefinido *a* / *an*, ni tampoco de un número.

rice (NO ~~a rice~~)
juice (NO ~~one juice~~)

Los sustantivos incontables suelen describir conceptos inmateriales como la vida (*life*) y el amor (*love*), y también cosas que no se pueden contar por unidades, por ejemplo, el agua (*water*), el pan (*bread*), el arroz (*rice*) o la leche (*milk*). Por eso se cuentan los vasos o litros de agua, las barras de pan, los granos de arroz, las cajas o botellas de leche, etc.

Siempre se utiliza *There is* ("hay") con los sustantivos incontables.

There's some bread on the table. Hay pan encima de la mesa.

### Spelling rules: plural nouns

**Reglas ortográficas: el plural de los sustantivos**

1 Normalmente el plural los sustantivos se forma añadiendo una *-s*.
apple / apples carrot / carrots

2 Los sustantivos que terminan en *-ch*, *-o*, *-sh* y *-x*, forman el plural añadiendo *-es*.
sandwich / sandwiches tomato / tomatoes
box / boxes dress / dresses

3 Si el sustantivo termina en consonante + *y*, la *-y* cambia a *-ies*.
strawberry / strawberries

## *some* and *any*

***some* y *any***

*Some* y *any* se utilizan con sustantivos contables e incontables.

There are some oranges but there isn't any butter. Hay algunas naranjas, pero no hay nada de mantequilla.

*Some* se utiliza en frases afirmativas. Significa "unos / as, algunos / as" con los sustantivos en plural, y "un poco de, algo de" con los sustantivos incontables.

I've got some potatoes. Tengo unas patatas.
She's got some rice. Tiene un poco de arroz.

*Any* se utiliza en frases negativas o interrogativas.

En las frases negativas, *any* significa "ningún / ninguna, nada de".

I haven't got any apples, and I haven't got any water. No tengo ninguna manzana y tampoco tengo nada de agua.

En las frases interrogativas, *any* significa "unos / as, algunos / as, algo de".

Have you got any apples and have you got any water? ¿Tienes unas manzanas? ¿Y algo de agua?

**! ¡Ojo!**

En las frases interrogativas se suele utilizar *any*, pero cuando se ofrece o se pide algo, también se puede utilizar *some*.

Do you want some biscuits? ¿Queréis galletas?
Would you like some orange juice? ¿Le apetece un zumo de naranja?
Can I have some milk, please? Quisiera un poco de leche, por favor.

## Indefinite pronouns

**Pronombres indefinidos**

### *someone* y *anyone*

Los pronombres indefinidos *someone* y *anyone* se utilizan para referirse a las personas.

En las frases afirmativas se utiliza *someone*, que significa "alguien".

There's someone in the living room. Hay alguien en el salón.

En las frases interrogativas se utiliza *anyone*. También significa "alguien".

Is there anyone in the classroom? ¿Hay alguien en la clase?

En las frases negativas *anyone* se traduce por "nadie".

There isn't anyone in the restaurant. No hay nadie en el restaurante.

### *something* y *anything*

Los pronombres indefinidos *something* y *anything* se utilizan para referirse a las cosas.

En las frases afirmativas se utiliza *something*, que significa "algo".

I want something to eat. Quiero comer algo.

En las frases interrogativas se utiliza *anything*. También significa "algo".

Is there anything to do? ¿Hay algo que hacer?

En las frases negativas *anything* se traduce por "nada".

Beatriz hasn't got anything to drink. Beatriz no tiene nada para beber.

### *some* / *someone* / *something* y *any* / *anyone* / *anything*

*Some* / *someone* / *something* se utilizan en las frases afirmativas.

*Any* / *anyone* / *anything* se utilizan en las frases negativas e interrogativas.

# Countable and uncountable nouns

**1 Are these nouns countable or uncountable? Write U or C.**

milk U
1 chip C
2 rice U
3 butter U

**2 Choose the correct options to complete the sentences.**

Can I have a hamburger? (pasta / hamburger)
1 I don't like cheese. (egg / cheese)
2 I'd like four drinks. (bread / drinks)
3 I'd like a sandwich. (chips / sandwich)
4 Can I have an orange? (orange / biscuit)

**3 Write the nouns in the plural.**

| | |
|---|---|
| chip | chips |
| 1 strawberry | strawberries |
| 2 orange | oranges |
| 3 box | boxes |
| 4 potato | potatoes |

# *some* and *any*

**4 Complete the sentences. Use *some* or *any*.**

Have you got any apples?
1 There aren't any eggs in the fridge.
2 'I'm thirsty.' 'Drink some water.'
3 We haven't got any coffee.
4 We've got some bananas in the bag.
5 Is there any jam in the cupboard?

**5 Write sentences with *There is / are* (affirmative or negative) and *a / an*, *some* or *any*.**

water ✓ There's some water.
oranges ✗ There aren't any oranges.
potato ✓ There's a potato.
1 bread ✗ There isn't any bread.
2 rice ✓ There's some rice.
3 carrot ✗ There isn't a carrot.
4 sandwich ✓ There's a sandwich.
5 egg ✓ There's an egg.

**6 Make the sentences in exercise 5 questions. Then write short answers. Use *Is there / Are there* and *a / an* or *any*.**

Is there any water?
Yes, there is.

Are there any oranges?
No, there aren't.

Is there a potato?
Yes, there is.

1 Is there any bread?
No, there isn't.
2 Is there any rice?
Yes, there is.
3 Is there a carrot?
No, there isn't.
4 Is there a sandwich?
Yes, there is.
5 Is there an egg?
Yes, there is.

**7 Complete the questions. Use *some* and *any*.**

Can I have some milk?
Is there any milk?
1 Have you got any cheese?
2 Would you like some cheese?
3 Do you want some chips?
4 Are there any chips?

# Indefinite pronouns

**8 Complete the sentences. Use *someone*, *anyone*, *something* and *anything*.**

Don't touch anything!
1 I'm thirsty but I haven't got anything to drink.
2 There's someone in the kitchen. Who is it?
3 Do you know anyone in Ireland?
4 Ow! I've got something in my eye!

## *be*: past simple

| Afirmativa | | |
|---|---|---|
| I was | | |
| you were | | |
| he was | she was | it was |
| we were | you were | they were |

*Was* se utiliza con la 1ª (*I*) y la 3ª (*he / she / it*) persona del singular, y *were* con las demás personas del verbo (*you / we / they*).

I was at the cinema. Estaba en el cine.

The exam was easy. El examen fue fácil.

We were at a concert last night. Anoche estuvimos en un concierto.

| Negativa | Formas contractas |
|---|---|
| I was not | I wasn't |
| you were not | you weren't |
| he was not | he wasn't |
| she was not | she wasn't |
| it was not | it wasn't |
| we were not | we weren't |
| you were not | you weren't |
| they were not | they weren't |

Para formar la negativa se coloca *not* detrás de *was, were*. Las formas contractas (*wasn't, weren't*) son más frecuentes.

The exam wasn't difficult. El examen no fue difícil.

They weren't at the shopping centre yesterday. Ayer no estaban en el centro comercial.

| Interrogativa | Respuestas breves | |
|---|---|---|
| | Afirmativa | Negativa |
| Was I …? | Yes, I was. | No, I wasn't. |
| Were you …? | Yes, you were. | No, you weren't. |
| Was he …? | Yes, he was. | No, he wasn't. |
| Was she …? | Yes, she was. | No, she wasn't. |
| Was it …? | Yes, it was. | No, it wasn't. |
| Were we …? | Yes, we were. | No, we weren't. |
| Were you …? | Yes, you were. | No, you weren't. |
| Were they …? | Yes, they were. | No, they weren't. |

La interrogativa se forma colocando *Was, Were* delante del sujeto.

Were you at school yesterday? ¿Ayer estabas en el colegio?

En la forma negativa de las respuestas breves se suelen utilizar las formas contractas (*wasn't, weren't*).

'Was Celia at the theatre last Saturday?' 'No, she wasn't.' "¿Estuvo Celia en el teatro el sábado pasado?" "No."

## Past time expressions

**Expresiones de pasado**

Al hablar del pasado se suelen utilizar expresiones con *last*.

last night anoche
last Saturday el sábado pasado
last week la semana pasada
last weekend el fin de semana pasado
last month el mes pasado
last July el pasado mes de julio
last year el año pasado
last winter el invierno pasado

También se utilizan otras expresiones para hablar del pasado.

yesterday ayer
yesterday morning ayer por la mañana
yesterday afternoon ayer por la tarde
the day before yesterday anteayer

## *there was / there were*

| | Afirmativa | Negativa | Interrogativa y respuestas breves |
|---|---|---|---|
| Singular | There was … | There was not …<br>Contracción: There wasn't … | Was there …?<br>Yes, there was. / No, there wasn't. |
| Plural | There were … | There were not …<br>Contracción: There weren't … | Were there …?<br>Yes, there were. / No, there weren't. |

*There was* y *there were* ("había / hubo") siguen las mismas reglas ortográficas que *there is / there's* y *there are*.

Consulta en la página 74 el uso de *there's* y *there are*.

En las frases negativas se suelen utilizar las formas contractas (*there wasn't, there weren't*).

En la forma negativa de las respuestas breves también se suelen usar las formas contractas (*there wasn't, there weren't*).

'Was there a concert yesterday?' 'No, there wasn't.' "¿Ayer hubo un concierto?" "No."

*There was, There wasn't* y *Was there* se utilizan con sustantivos en singular.

There was some milk in the fridge. Había un poco de leche en el frigorífico.
There wasn't a teacher in the classroom. No había ningun profesor en clase.
Was there any cheese on the table? ¿Había queso encima de la mesa?

*There were, There weren't* y *Were there* se utilizan con sustantivos en plural.

There were some books on the desk. Había algunos libros encima del escritorio.
There weren't any children at the museum. No había ningún niño en el museo.
Were there any apples in your bag? ¿Había alguna manzana en tu bolsa?

Consulta en la página 76 los sustantivos contables e incontables, y también el uso de *some* y *any*.

## *be*: past simple

**1 Complete the sentences. Use the affirmative or negative past simple of *be*.**

The music festival wasn't very good. It was terrible.

1 It wasn't Tuesday yesterday. It was Wednesday.

2 My dad wasn't in Brighton last week. He was in Cambridge.

3 My friends were at the shopping centre. They weren't in the park.

4 The sandwiches weren't on the table. They were in the fridge.

**2 Write questions and short answers. Use the past simple of *be*.**

Tom / at the stadium / yesterday? ✓
Was Tom at the stadium yesterday?
Yes, he was.

1 your friends / at the theatre last night? ✓
Were your friends at the theatre last night?
Yes, they were.

2 your sister / at the swimming pool? ✗
Was your sister at the swimming pool?
No, she wasn't.

3 the art gallery / interesting? ✗
Was the art gallery interesting?
No, it wasn't.

4 the students / at the museum? ✗
Were the students at the museum?
No, they weren't.

5 the weather / hot yesterday? ✓
Was the weather hot yesterday?
Yes, it was.

**3 Put the time expressions in the correct order.**

a) the day before yesterday 5
b) last month 2
c) last weekend 4
d) yesterday morning 6
e) yesterday afternoon 7
f) last night 8
g) last year 1
h) last week 3

## *there was / there were*

**4 Read the list of food and drinks for a party. Write sentences with *There was* and *There were*.**

| | |
|---|---|
| *sandwiches* | *fruit* |
| *a big pizza* | *six bottles of cola* |
| *chips* | *a chocolate cake* |

There were some sandwiches.

1 There was a big pizza.
2 There were some chips.
3 There was some fruit.
4 There were six bottles of cola.
5 There was a chocolate cake.

**5 Complete the sentences. Use *There wasn't* and *There weren't*.**

There weren't any good CDs at the music shop.

1 There wasn't any bread at the baker's.
2 There wasn't a nice jumper at the clothes shop.
3 There weren't any people at the bus station.
4 There wasn't any milk on the table.

**6 Write questions and short answers. Use *Was there / Were there* and *a* or *any*.**

cola / in the fridge? ✓
Was there any cola in the fridge?
Yes, there was.

1 music festival / in the park? ✗
Was there a music festival in the park?
No, there wasn't.

2 water / in your bag? ✗
Was there any water in your bag?
No, there wasn't.

3 nice postcards / at the post office? ✓
Were there any nice postcards at the post office?
Yes, there were.

4 statues / at the museum? ✗
Were there any statues at the museum?
No, there weren't.

5 food / at the party ✓
Was there any food at the party?
Yes, there was.

## Past simple affirmative (regular verbs)

***Past simple* afirmativa (verbos regulares)**

| Afirmativa |
| --- |
| I watched<br>you watched<br>he watched<br>she watched<br>it watched<br>we watched<br>you watched<br>they watched |

La forma del pasado de los verbos regulares es la misma para todas las personas del verbo.

### Spelling rules: past simple affirmative (regular verbs)

**Reglas ortográficas: *past simple* afirmativa (verbos regulares)**

1 Con la mayoría de los verbos, se añade *-ed* al infinitivo del verbo sin *to*.
start / started visit / visited watch / watched

2 Con verbos acabados en *-e*, se añade *-d*.
dance / danced like / liked arrive / arrived

3 Con verbos acabados en *-y*, la *-y* se sustituye por *-ied*.
carry / carried study / studied
Excepción: play / played

4 Con verbos acabados en una consonante precedida de una sola vocal, la consonante se duplica y se añade *-ed*.
stop /stopped chat / chatted

## Past simple affirmative (irregular verbs)

***Past simple* afirmativa (verbos irregulares)**

Hay verbos que son irregulares y no forman el pasado añadiendo *-ed* al infinitivo sin *to*. La forma es la misma para todas las personas del verbo.

go (ir) / went (I went, you went, he went, we went, etc.)

Estos verbos no siguen reglas ortográficas específicas. Hay que aprendérselos de memoria.

Ejemplos: see (ver) / saw
buy (comprar) / bought
have (tener) / had

Consulta la lista de verbos irregulares en el interior de la contraportada.

### Usos

Utilizamos el *past simple* para hablar de acciones que tuvieron lugar en un momento determinado del pasado, por ejemplo, anoche (*last night*), ayer (*yesterday*), el año pasado (*last year*), etc.

I played basketball last Sunday. El domingo pasado jugué al baloncesto.
We went to Madrid last summer. El verano pasado fuimos a Madrid.

## Adverbs of manner

**Adverbios de modo**

Indican cómo se desarrolla una acción. Los adverbios regulares se forman añadiendo *-ly* a los adjetivos. Los adjetivos terminados en *-y* cambian a *-ily*.

slow (lento / a) / slowly (lentamente)

happy (feliz, alegre) / happily (felizmente, alegremente)

Hay adverbios irregulares que hay que aprender de memoria.

good (bueno / a) / well (bien)

fast (rápido / a) – fast (rápidamente)

straight (recto / a, directo) / straight (en línea recta, directamente)

## Past simple affirmative (regular verbs)

**1 Complete the sentences. Use the past simple forms of the verbs in the box.**

dance play start study visit ~~watch~~

We watched videos on YouTube last night.
1 The concert started at three o'clock.
2 Last summer I visited Elvis Presley's home.
3 They danced to pop music at Nicole's party.
4 I played the guitar after school.
5 Paul studied a lot for his maths exam.

**2 Complete the sentences. Use the past simple forms of the verbs in the brackets.**

John practised (practise) the guitar yesterday morning.
1 They chatted (chat) on the phone for two hours.
2 We arrived (arrive) home late last night.
3 I carried (carry) my grandma's bag.
4 The bus stopped (stop) in front of the supermarket.
5 She studied (study) for three hours.

## Past simple affirmative (irregular verbs)

**3 Write the base forms of the past simple verbs.**

bought buy
1 saw see
2 met meet
3 heard hear
4 went go
5 had have

**4 Write the past simple forms. Use the list of irregular verbs inside the back cover to help you.**

read read
1 fly flew
2 do did
3 meet met
4 sleep slept
5 leave left
6 write wrote
7 sing sang

**5 Complete the sentences. Use the verbs from exercise 4.**

I read a very good book last week.
1 Marta wrote an email to Rob yesterday.
2 Chris and Beth met in a café at 10:30 a.m.
3 Tony and Ann left here at one o'clock.
4 I sang at a concert last weekend.
5 We did a puzzle last night.
6 Lisa slept at my house last night.
7 My uncle flew to Barcelona last Monday.

## Past simple affirmative (regular and irregular verbs)

**6 Complete the paragraph. Use the past simple forms of the verbs in brackets.**

Last Saturday I went (go) to a concert with my friend, Megan. We saw (**1** see) Maroon 5. It was brilliant. The concert finished (**2** finish) at half past nine. After the concert we had (**3** have) dinner in a café. We ate (**4** eat) pizza and drank (**5** drink) cola. Then we walked (**6** walk) home and watched (**7** watch) some music videos.

## Adverbs of manner

**7 Complete the sentences. Use the adverbs in the box.**

~~beautifully~~ correctly fast slowly well

Greg plays the saxophone very beautifully.
1 Can you speak more slowly, please?
2 You answered all the exam questions correctly.
3 My brother can run very fast.
4 Stopa played really well at the concert. It was great!

## *going to*

| Afirmativa | Formas contractas |
|---|---|
| I am going to eat | I'm going to eat |
| you are going to eat | you're going to eat |
| he is going to eat<br>she is going to eat<br>it is going to eat | he's going to eat<br>she's going to eat<br>it's going to eat |
| we are going to eat<br>you are going to eat<br>they are going to eat | we're going to eat<br>you're going to eat<br>they're going to eat |

El futuro con *going to* se forma con el *present simple* del auxiliar *be* con *going to* y el infinitivo sin *to* del verbo principal. Significa "ir a hacer algo".

I'm going to travel with my friends this summer. Este verano voy a viajar con mis amigos.

| Negativa | Formas contractas |
|---|---|
| I am not going to eat | I'm not going to eat |
| you are not going to eat | you aren't going to eat |
| he is not going to eat<br>she is not going to eat<br>it is not going to eat | he isn't going to eat<br>she isn't going to eat<br>it isn't going to eat |
| we are not going to eat<br>you are not going to eat<br>they are not going to eat | we aren't going to eat<br>you aren't going to eat<br>they aren't going to eat |

La negativa se forma colocando *not* detrás del auxiliar *be*. Las formas contractas son más frecuentes.

We aren't going to sleep in a tent. No vamos a dormir en una tienda de campaña.

| Interrogativa | Respuestas breves | |
|---|---|---|
| | Afirmativa | Negativa |
| Am I going to eat? | Yes, I am. | No, I'm not. |
| Are you going to eat? | Yes, you are. | No, you aren't. |
| Is he going to eat? | Yes, he is. | No, he isn't. |
| Is she going to eat? | Yes, she is. | No, she isn't. |
| Is it going to eat? | Yes, it is. | No, it isn't. |
| Are we going to eat? | Yes, we are. | No, we aren't. |
| Are you going to eat? | Yes, you are. | No, you aren't. |
| Are they going to eat? | Yes, they are. | No, they aren't. |

La interrogativa se forma colocando *Am*, *Are*, *Is* delante del sujeto.

Are you going to visit us next summer? ¿Nos vais a visitar el verano que viene?

En las respuestas breves, el verbo principal (*playing*, *eating*, etc.) se omite, y se utiliza únicamente el auxiliar *be*.

'Is he going to buy a map?' 'Yes, he is.' "¿Va a comprar un mapa?" "Sí."

En las respuestas breves negativas se suelen utilizar las formas contractas (*'m not*, *aren't*, *isn't*).

'Are they going to stay with you?' 'No, they aren't.' "¿Se van a quedar con vosotros?" "No."

### Usos

*Going to* se utiliza para hablar de planes y de cosas que hemos decidido hacer.

Next summer we're going to visit Paris. El próximo verano vamos a visitar París.

I'm not going to see a film this evening. Esta noche no voy a ver una película.

Are you going to play basketball on Sunday? ¿Vas a jugar al baloncesto el domingo?

### Future time expressions

**Expresiones de futuro**

Para hablar del futuro se suelen utilizar expresiones con *next*.

next Saturday / month / year el sábado / mes / año que viene
next week la semana que viene
next weekend el próximo fin de semana
next August el próximo mes de agosto
next summer el próximo verano

También se utilizan otras expresiones para hablar del futuro.

tomorrow mañana
tomorrow morning mañana por la mañana
tomorrow afternoon mañana por la tarde
the day after tomorrow pasado mañana

## Present continuous with future meaning

***Present continuous* con valor de futuro**

El *present continuous* se puede utilizar para describir planes de futuro. Este tipo de frases suele incluir expresiones temporales, por ejemplo, *tomorrow*.

What are they doing next weekend? ¿Qué van a hacer el próximo fin de semana?

I'm visiting my cousins on Sunday. El domingo voy a visitar a mis primos.

## *must / mustn't*

La forma *must* es la misma para todas las personas del verbo.

I must, you must, he / she / it must, we must, you must, they must

*Must* y *mustn't* se utilizan con el infinitivo sin *to* del verbo principal.

We must turn left. (NO ~~We must to turn left.~~) Tenemos que girar a la izquierda.

La negativa se forma colocando *not* detrás de *must*. La forma contracta (*mustn't*) es más frecuente. Las formas *must not* y *mustn't* son las mismas para todas las personas del verbo.

You mustn't talk loudly in hospitals. No debes hablar alto en los hospitales.

### Usos

1 *Must* expresa la obligación o la necesidad de hacer algo. *Mustn't* expresa prohibición.
You must be quiet in the library. Debes guardar silencio en la biblioteca.
We mustn't use our phones in class. No debemos usar nuestros teléfonos en clase.

2 *Must* y *mustn't* se pueden utilizar para dar un consejo o hacer una recomendación seria.
It's a fantastic film! You must see it! ¡Es un libro fantástico! ¡Debes leerlo!
You mustn't smoke. It's bad for you. No debes fumar. Es muy malo para la salud.

3 *Must* también se utiliza para expresar que nos sentimos obligados a hacer una cosa.
I must go home now. It's very late. Debo irme a casa. Es muy tarde.
I must do my homework before dinner. Tengo que hacer los deberes antes de cenar.

## *going to*

**1 Write affirmative sentences. Use *going to*.**

I / visit my grandparents in Dublin
I'm going to visit my grandparents in Dublin.

1 she / buy a new swimsuit
She's going to buy a new swimsuit.

2 we / learn French next year
We're going to learn French next year.

3 I / play hockey on Saturday
I'm going to play hockey on Saturday.

**2 Make the sentences in exercise 1 negative.**

I'm not going to visit my grandparents in Dublin.

1 She's not going to buy a new swimsuit.
2 We're not going to learn French next year.
3 I'm not going to play hockey on Saturday.

**3 Complete the paragraph. Use *going to*.**

This weekend I'm going to visit (visit) my cousins in London. I 'm not going to take (**1** not take) the train. I 'm going to go (**2** go) by bus. My aunt 's going to meet (**3** meet) me at the bus station. On Saturday we 're going to visit (**4** visit) the Tower of London. My aunt isn't going to come (**5** not come) with us.

**4 Philip, Dan and Ed are going to London. Write questions and short answers about their plans.**

| | Philip | Dan and Ed |
|---|---|---|
| visit museums | ✗ | (2) ✓ |
| stay in a hotel | (1) ✓ | (3) ✗ |

Philip / visit museums?
Is Philip going to visit museums?
No, he isn't.

1 Philip / stay in a hotel?
Is Philip going to stay in a hotel?
Yes, he is.

2 Dan and Ed / visit museums?
Are Dan and Ed going to visit museums?
Yes, they are.

3 Dan and Ed / stay in a hotel?
Are Dan and Ed going to stay in a hotel?
No, they aren't.

**5 Put the time expressions in the correct order. (Imagine that today is Monday.)**

a) next week 5
b) tomorrow morning 1
c) next weekend 4
d) next month 6
e) the day after tomorrow 2
f) next Friday 3

## Present continuous with future meaning

**6 Put the words in the correct order to write sentences.**

train / aren't / tomorrow. / the / We / taking
We aren't taking the train tomorrow.

1 the / Is / museum / she / later? / visiting
Is she visiting the museum later?

2 I / cinema / am / tonight. / to / going / the
I am going to the cinema tonight.

3 a / are / hotel. / in / small / staying / They
They are staying in a small hotel.

4 the / He / isn't / to / beach / next / weekend. / coming
He isn't coming to the beach next weekend.

## *must / mustn't*

**7 Rewrite the sentences. Use *must* or *mustn't*.**

Don't forget your passport.
You mustn't forget your passport.

1 Don't be late for the aeroplane.
You mustn't be late for the aeroplane.

2 Take your sunglasses.
You must take your sunglasses.

3 Don't stay out late at night.
You mustn't stay out late at night.

4 Put on suncream at the beach.
You must put on suncream at the beach.

## Words to learn

### Faces

dark ______
ear ______
eye ______
fair ______
freckles ______
glasses ______
hair ______
long ______
mouth ______
nose ______
short ______
teeth ______

### Family

aunt ______
brother ______
cousin ______
daughter ______
father ______
grandfather ______
grandmother ______
grandparents ______
husband ______
mother ______
parents ______
sister ______
son ______
uncle ______
wife ______

## Phrases to learn

Can I borrow it, please? ______
Sorry. ______
Of course. Here you are. ______

## 1

**Follow the labyrinth. Find the words about faces.**

| Start → | e | s | Finish |
|---|---|---|---|
| e | y | e | s |
| m | o | a | s |
| t | u | l | g |
| h | h | a | r |
| i | a | e | s |
| r | n | l | e |
| s | o | k | c |
| e | f | r | e |

Which word is missing?

Which word is not a body part?

## 2

**Which letters are missing from the alphabet? Put them in the correct order to make adjectives for hair.**

AXHSFQJPEDIWMRCTVKBYUZ

GLNO = long

1 NZCGXAFWQIBLDUYMKEPJV

2 GZBUMWTFPIXSQCYNVLJEHO

3 BXMTVEGOYSNLWPUKZQCHDJ

## 3

**Read about Alex. Where is he on the family tree?**

His grandparents have got three children.

His aunt and uncle have got two sons and a daughter.

He's got two sisters and a brother.

He hasn't got long hair.

## 4

**Read about Alex's family. Then match the names and the pictures of Alex's family in puzzle 3.**

Allie Bill Chris Danny
Helen Ian Jake Jemima
Joanna Lily Philip
Sarah Simon

*What's **your** dad's name? What's **your** mum's name?*

Hi! I'm Alex, and this is my family. My grandfather's name is Philip. His wife, Joanna, is my grandmother. My grandma and grandpa are cool! They're the parents of three children. They've got two sons, Ian and Chris, and their daughter, Allie, is my mother. My uncle Ian hasn't got a wife and he isn't a father. Chris is Helen's husband. My cousins are Lily, Danny and Simon. Simon's got short hair, and Danny's got long hair. He's my favourite cousin. I've got two sisters, Jemima and Sarah, and a brother, Bill. Sarah is the only girl in our family with fair hair. She's got freckles too!

Answers: see Teacher's Guide

## Words to learn

### Free-time activities

chat on the Internet ____________
do puzzles ____________
go skateboarding ____________
go to the cinema ____________
listen to music ____________
make models ____________
meet friends ____________
play computer games ____________
play the piano ____________
read magazines ____________
talk on the phone ____________
watch TV ____________

### Sports

aerobics ____________
athletics ____________
basketball ____________
cycling ____________
football ____________
gymnastics ____________
hockey ____________
ice skating ____________
martial arts ____________
skiing ____________
swimming ____________
tennis ____________
volleyball ____________
water polo ____________
windsurfing ____________

## Phrases to learn

I'm bored! ____________
Let's go (to the cinema). ____________
What time is it now? ____________
Let's meet (at the cinema) at (six o'clock). ____________
See you there. ____________

## 1

**Copy the letters with the same colour and put the letters in the correct order. Then complete the sentences about Gemma.**

| | | | | | | |
|---|---|---|---|---|---|---|
| t | o | r | l | i | a | e |
| e | t | s | a | c | d | a |
| m | a | k | s | c | s | l |
| e | e | s | e | p | e | m |
| w | y | t | e | h | n | h |
| s | d | s | o | l | s | a |
| e | s | g | t | t | k | a |

Gemma ielsnst to music on her MP3 player.
Gemma listens to music on her MP3 player.

1. She ___ to the cinema on Saturdays.
2. Does she ___ to her boyfriend on the phone?
3. Gemma and her friends often ___ computer games.
4. She never ___ puzzles.
5. She ___ friends at her favourite café.
6. She ___ with her friend on the Internet.
7. Does she ___ fashion magazines?
8. Gemma never ___ models.
9. She ___ TV in her bedroom after school.

## 2

**Copy every second letter. What are the messages?**

Msikkaetoefbtoeanrgdoiensg

*Mike often goes skateboarding.*

1. Ilsaoymtehteipmieasnpo.
2. DgooesswJiamvmiienrg?
3. Iwcaatnetrpploalyo.

## 3

**SOLVE THE CODE TO FIND THE ACTIVITIES.**

| a | b | c | d | e | f | g | h | i |
|---|---|---|---|---|---|---|---|---|
| g | | i | | k | | m | | o |
| **j** | **k** | **l** | **m** | **n** | **o** | **p** | **q** | **r** |
| | q | | s | | u | | w | |
| **s** | **t** | **u** | **v** | **w** | **x** | **y** | **z** | |
| y | | a | | c | | e | | |

| 1 play | 2 go | 3 do |
|---|---|---|
| piffysvuff (volleyball) | wswfcha | gulncuf ulnm |
| ziinvuff | mqcggcha | uylivcwm |
| vumeynvuff | cwy meuncha | unbfyncwm |
| nyhhcm | qchxmolzcha | asghumncwm |
| | meccha | |

How often do you do these activities?

## 4

**Copy the words with the same colour. Put the words in the correct order to make sentences.**

| | |
|---|---|
| I | goes |
| my | gymnastics |
| teacher | can't |
| do | play |
| volleyball | my |
| play | can |
| I | friends |
| skiing | hockey |

Are the sentences true for you?

Answers: see Teacher's Guide

# Words to learn

## Weekday routine

do homework ______
finish classes ______
get dressed ______
get up ______
go home ______
go to bed ______
have a break ______
have a shower ______
have breakfast ______
have dinner ______
have lunch ______
leave home ______
start classes ______

## School subjects

art ______
boring ______
difficult ______
easy ______
English ______
French ______
fun ______
geography ______
history ______
ICT ______
interesting ______
maths ______
music ______
PE ______
science ______
technology ______

# Phrases to learn

I like … ______
I don't like / I dislike … ______
I love … ______
I hate … ______
Do you like (English)? ______
I think it's (fun). ______

## 1 Do the crossword.

→

1 I usually leave ________ at about 8:15 a.m.
2 I ________ lunch at school.
3 At 10 p.m., I go ________ bed.
4 I ________ home from school at 4 p.m.
5 I have ________ with my mum and dad at 7:45 a.m.
6 At about 7:30 a.m., I get ________ in my school clothes.

↓

7 I always have a ________ after I get up.
8 I usually do ________ before I watch TV.
9 I start ________ at 9 a.m. and finish them at 3:45 p.m.

## 2 Follow the labyrinth. Find the school subjects.

## 3 Which letters are missing from the alphabet? Put them in the correct order to see what the students think.

C G R O W F X H T I K J L V N D Z P Q B M U → AESY

1 M Y C J E F X L W V S P Z A Q K D T H U

2 V A N W G K S Z O J P E X B R Q H Y M

3 O A M Y D F X H Z K L V C B P Q W U J

4 M J A D O S H Z E K R W G V T I B Y L Q X C P

**Michelle** thinks PE and science are really *easy*.

1 **Bruno** thinks maths is __ __ __ __ __ __ __.
2 **Sanjit** doesn't speak English at home, so he thinks it is __ __ f __ i __ __ __ __.
3 For **Alicia**, art is the only __ n __ __ __ e __ t i __ __ subject.
4 **Hugo** thinks music is __ __ __.

## 4 SOLVE THE CODE. WHAT ARE THE QUESTIONS?

| a | b | c | d | e | f | g | h | i |
|---|---|---|---|---|---|---|---|---|
| e | f | g | h | i | j | k | l | m |
| j | k | l | m | n | o | p | q | r |
| n | o | p | q | r | s | t | u | v |
| s | t | u | v | w | x | y | z | |
| w | x | y | z | a | b | c | d | |

**DKS KHZ WNA UKQ?**

*How old are you?*

1 **SDANA ZK UKQ ZK UKQN DKIASKNG?**
2 **SDWP YHWOO ZK UKQ DWRA WP JEJA?**
3 **SDAJ ZK UKQ CAP QL?**
4 **SDK EO UKQN DEOPKNU PAWYDAN?**
5 **ZK UKQ DWRA W XNAWG WBPAN UKQ DWRA ZEJJAN?**

Answer the questions for you.

## Words to learn

### Weather

It's cloudy. ______

It's cold. ______

It's cool. ______

It's foggy. ______

It's hot. ______

It's icy. ______

It's rainy. ______

It's snowy. ______

It's stormy. ______

It's sunny. ______

It's warm. ______

It's windy. ______

### Clothes

boots ______

coat ______

dress ______

jacket ______

jeans ______

jumper ______

raincoat ______

sandals ______

scarf ______

shirt ______

shoes ______

shorts ______

skirt ______

socks ______

trainers ______

trousers ______

## Phrases to learn

What's the weather like? ______

Can I help you? ______

How much is this (umbrella)? ______

I'd like this (umbrella), please. ______

Here you are. ______

Here's your change. ______

# 1 Complete the world weather report.

| | | | | | | | |
|---|---|---|---|---|---|---|---|
| a | u | y | o | w | t | r | y |
| y | f | r | r | y | n | u | o |
| h | d | l | n | n | l | g | t |
| o | c | o | y | s | m | s | d |
| y | m | w | a | d | i | w | i |
| n | n | o | s | g | y | c | o |

Put the red letters in order to find two extra words.

Hello, and welcome to the weather report. The weather is different everywhere today! In Spain, it's sunny, and in Greece, it's ___ – nearly 35°C! It's ___ in France, but in Japan it's really ___ – only 8°C. In Canada, it's ___ and people are skiing. They're wearing jumpers in Italy – it's very ___ – and in China it's ___ too. They've got umbrellas in England, because it's ___, and in Portugal, it's ___, so it's a good idea to stay indoors. In the USA, it's very ___. So the weather is changing all the time!

# 2 Name the boys. There is one name that you don't need.

Ben Dan Mike Sam

Dan's wearing green.
Mike's jacket is red.
Sam and Mike aren't wearing green.
Sam and Dan's jackets are blue.
Ben and Mike are wearing trainers.
Dan and Sam are wearing boots.

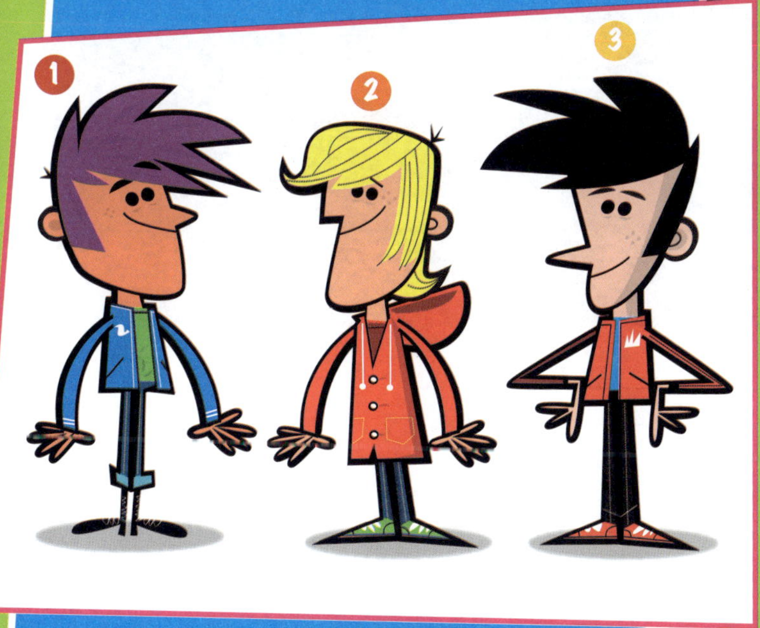


# 3 Follow the lines. Complete the lists.

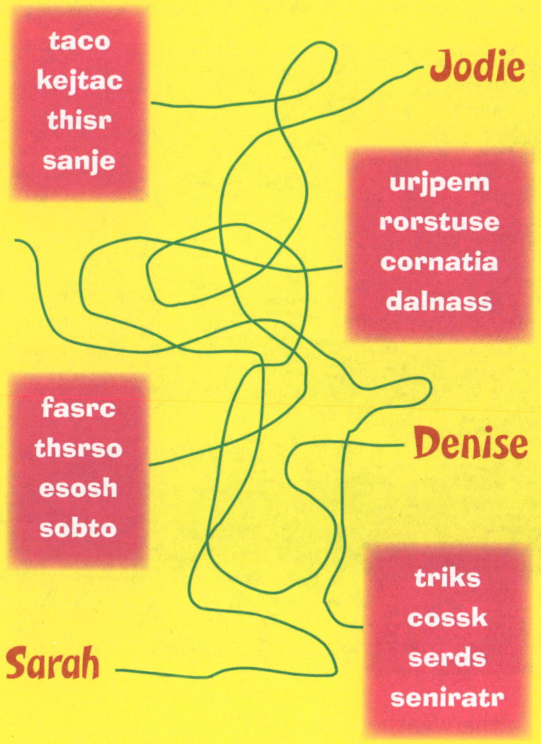


1 Denise wants *a coat*, ..., ... and ... .
2 Sarah wants ..., ..., ... and ... .
3 Jodie wants ..., ..., ... and ... .
4 Nobody wants ..., ..., ... and ... .

## Words to learn

| Places at home | | Furniture | |
|---|---|---|---|
| balcony | ______ | armchair | ______ |
| bathroom | ______ | bath | ______ |
| bedroom | ______ | bedside table | ______ |
| dining room | ______ | bookcase | ______ |
| garage | ______ | chest of drawers | ______ |
| garden | ______ | cooker | ______ |
| hall | ______ | cupboard | ______ |
| kitchen | ______ | fridge | ______ |
| living room | ______ | lamp | ______ |
| patio | ______ | mirror | ______ |
| stairs | ______ | shelf | ______ |
| toilet | ______ | sink | ______ |
| | | sofa | ______ |
| | | stool | ______ |
| | | wardrobe | ______ |

## Phrases to learn

It's (Paul). ______

Can I speak to (Jason), please? ______

I'm sorry. ______

Can (he) call you back in ten minutes? ______

## 1

Find the letters with the same colours. Put them in order to find nine places in a home.

RGOMDNIINO = dining room

Which three places are missing?

| | | | | | | | | | |
|---|---|---|---|---|---|---|---|---|---|
| R | I | K | G | O | E | O | E | M | A |
| H | S | R | A | C | L | O | B | A | D |
| A | E | N | O | R | I | Y | T | H | G |
| C | I | L | A | A | R | G | I | A | N |
| T | B | G | R | E | H | T | L | O | D |
| I | T | M | O | N | T | L | N | S | N |

## 2

**Solve the code. Answer the questions.**

| 1 | 2 | 3 | 4 | 5 | 6 | 7 | 8 | 9 | 10 | 11 | 12 | 13 |
|---|---|---|---|---|---|---|---|---|---|---|---|---|
| e | f | g | h | i | j | k | l | m | n | o | p | q |
| 14 | 15 | 16 | 17 | 18 | 19 | 20 | 21 | 22 | 23 | 24 | 25 | 26 |
| r | s | t | u | v | w | x | y | z | a | b | c | d |

5·15 16·4·1·14·1 23 3·23·14·26·1·10 23·16 21·11·17·14 4·11·9·1?

Is there a garden at your home?

1 19·4·23·16 2·17·14·10·5·16·17·14·1 5·15 16·4·1·14·1?

2 23·14·1 16·4·1·14·1 15·16·23·5·14·15 5·10 21·11·17·14 4·11·9·1?

3 5·15 16·4·1·14·1 23 24·23·16·4 5·10 21·11·17·14 24·23·16·4·14·11·11·9?

4 19·4·5·25·4 14·11·11·9·15 4·23·18·1 3·11·16 24·11·11·7·25·23·15·1·15 5·10 16·4·1·9?

## 3

**Find fifteen pieces of furniture.**

| | | | | | | | | | | | | | |
|---|---|---|---|---|---|---|---|---|---|---|---|---|---|
| H | T | S | Q | P | U | D | C | O | W | T | P | E | R |
| G | E | F | N | P | W | O | U | E | K | B | A | T | H |
| E | B | R | J | L | A | M | P | I | H | Y | G | C | N |
| D | Q | I | T | W | P | N | B | F | R | M | B | O | H |
| A | O | D | I | W | S | T | O | M | I | R | R | O | R |
| R | L | G | F | Y | B | O | A | B | T | E | L | K | O |
| M | Y | E | C | D | O | Q | R | E | J | S | Y | E | M |
| C | H | E | S | T | O | F | D | R | A | W | E | R | S |
| H | K | M | G | L | K | E | C | X | S | I | F | W | O |
| A | S | U | E | W | C | S | H | U | T | R | A | H | F |
| I | I | N | G | W | A | R | D | R | O | B | E | X | A |
| R | N | W | R | P | S | G | D | M | O | A | K | Q | E |
| P | K | H | T | B | E | S | H | E | L | F | C | I | G |
| H | C | B | E | D | S | I | D | E | T | A | B | L | E |

## 4

Find two words in every room. Use all the letters.

balcony, fridge

## Words to learn

| Breakfast | | Lunch and dinner | |
|---|---|---|---|
| apple juice | ________ | carrots | ________ |
| bacon | ________ | chicken | ________ |
| biscuits | ________ | chips | ________ |
| bread | ________ | chocolate cake | ________ |
| butter | ________ | fish | ________ |
| cereal | ________ | green salad | ________ |
| cheese | ________ | hamburgers | ________ |
| eggs | ________ | ice cream | ________ |
| fruit | ________ | pasta | ________ |
| honey | ________ | peas | ________ |
| jam | ________ | potatoes | ________ |
| milk | ________ | rice | ________ |
| orange juice | ________ | roast beef | ________ |
| toast | ________ | sandwiches | ________ |
| yoghurt | ________ | strawberries | ________ |

## Phrases to learn

What do you have (for breakfast)? ________

What's for breakfast? ________

Can I take your order? ________

I'd like (a chicken sandwich), please. ________

And to drink? ________

Anything else? ________

## 1 Who has which breakfast? Write the correct names. There is one name you don't need.

Dave Emily Fred Katie

Fred and Katie have eggs for breakfast.

Everyone has toast. Katie, Emily and Dave have jam on it.

Emily and one of the men have cereal.

Dave and Katie love bacon for breakfast.

Emily doesn't like yoghurt.

Nobody drinks tea, but Dave and Katie have apple juice.

## 2 Use the letters to make nine foods.

| | | | | | | |
|---|---|---|---|---|---|---|
| b | u | t | c | h | i | c |
| c | a | r | r | b | i | s |
| f | r | u | l | k | e | y |
| t | e | r | t | o | e | s |
| p | o | o | t | s | i | t |
| m | i | h | o | n | s | e |
| c | h | e | e | k | e | n |
| c | u | i | t | s | t | a |

Put these letters in order to find two more foods.

**regaebdsdrleaan**

## 3 Which letters of the alphabet are missing? Put them in order to find what the people have for dinner.

J Z E F O R Y L V K B P T X Q M U G

2 T A N C E V J R Z G O Q B L D W M X P K U Y

1 D F J S U W K P Z G V L H Y B X Q O N T

3 Z C I N U G J V H M P K Y D L W Q X

**Paul** has a sandwich.

1 **Bruce** has __ c __ __ __ e __ __ for dessert.

2 **Claudia** loves __ __ __ __.

3 **Georgia's** favourite is __ __ __ __ __ __ __ e __.

## 4 Write six differences between picture A and picture B.

A: hamburger, B: chocolate cake

A

B

## Words to learn

| Places in town (1) | | Places in town (2) | |
|---|---|---|---|
| airport | ______ | baker's | ______ |
| art gallery | ______ | bus stop | ______ |
| bridge | ______ | chemist's | ______ |
| bus station | ______ | clothes shop | ______ |
| cinema | ______ | library | ______ |
| concert hall | ______ | music shop | ______ |
| hospital | ______ | pedestrian crossing | ______ |
| museum | ______ | police station | ______ |
| palace | ______ | post office | ______ |
| river | ______ | sports centre | ______ |
| shopping centre | ______ | supermarket | ______ |
| stadium | ______ | swimming pool | ______ |
| theatre | ______ | | |
| train station | ______ | | |

## Phrases to learn

Excuse me. ______

Is there (a chemist's) near here? ______

How do I get there? ______

Go straight on. ______

Turn (right / left). ______

It's opposite (the hospital). ______

## 1

Read about the town where Sarah grew up. Match the places with their names. There are two places that you don't need.

*baker's chemist's cinema library museum post office shopping centre*

There were shops on the left and the right of the baker's.
The post office was opposite the museum.
There wasn't a shop on the left of the shopping centre.
There weren't any shops on the left or the right of the post office.
There was a cinema on the right of the shopping centre.
There was a baker's on the right of the library.
The chemist's was opposite the shopping centre.

## 2

**Find twelve places.**

| | | | | | | | | | | | | |
|---|---|---|---|---|---|---|---|---|---|---|---|---|
| G | C | O | N | C | E | R | T | H | A | L | L | T |
| T | E | U | S | R | F | O | E | R | I | V | E | R |
| B | A | R | T | G | A | L | L | E | R | Y | W | A |
| U | W | Y | W | T | D | I | Q | U | T | Q | R | I |
| S | W | I | M | M | I | N | G | P | O | O | L | N |
| S | R | D | B | H | R | B | Y | H | P | Y | F | S |
| T | A | S | U | E | K | G | R | T | S | B | D | T |
| A | F | T | S | U | B | S | L | H | E | R | M | A |
| T | I | A | S | O | A | E | I | E | J | I | P | T |
| I | E | D | T | G | K | Q | B | A | R | D | G | I |
| O | J | I | O | T | E | L | E | T | A | G | E | O |
| N | S | U | P | E | R | M | A | R | K | E | T | N |
| O | R | M | U | A | S | W | M | E | T | F | Y | E |

**Which two extra places can you find in the green letters?**

## 3

**Copy every second letter. What are the messages?**

Itsstnheearreyaocuhrehmoimse?
*Is there a chemist's near your home?*

1 Wahviocuhriistyeosuhrofp?

2 Asrceetnhterreesanneyasrphoerrte?

3 Wmhuasteiusmtyhoeubkensotw?

**Answer the questions for you and your town.**

## 4

**Follow the labyrinth. Find the places.**

| Start → c | | g | Finish |
|---|---|---|---|
| o | l | n | i |
| t | h | s | s |
| s | e | o | r |
| s | h | n | c |
| p | o | a | i |
| h | o | t | r |
| p | s | s | e |
| i | t | e | d |
| l | a | p | m |
| p | a | i | u |
| a | l | d | a |
| c | e | s | t |

Which three extra places can you find in the green, orange and blue letters?

## Words to learn

**Types of music**

classical ______
country ______
fast ______
flamenco ______
gospel ______
heavy metal ______
hip hop ______
jazz ______
loud ______
opera ______
pop ______
quiet ______
reggae ______
rock ______
salsa ______
slow ______

**Musical instruments**

cello ______
clarinet ______
cymbals ______
drums ______
flute ______
guitar ______
harp ______
saxophone ______
tambourine ______
triangle ______
trombone ______
trumpet ______
violin ______
xylophone ______

## Phrases to learn

Let's buy a present for (her). ______
Why don't we get (Kasabian's new CD)? ______
Shall we get (Coldplay's new CD)? ______
That's a great idea! ______

# 1 Who plays which instrument? Who plays nothing?

1 Nia plays … .
2 Liam plays … .
3 Tito plays … .
4 Lisa plays … .
5 Harvey plays … .

# 2 Find two words in each box. Use all the letters.

| | | |
|---|---|---|
| n t o l r o i<br>i y c u v n | 1 r o r e a p<br>a e g g e | 2 t a z a n z<br>j u b o r i e m |
| 3 e e h e l n y h<br>t p a o x m a o v y l | 4 s t s o n r<br>m b o l a a e | 5 g a a c r i t i a<br>l l n e s s c l |
| 6 s e o e p o<br>l c l l g | 7 p m h l c o<br>a r a f e n | 8 p i h k o<br>h c o r p |

country, violin

# 3

*Who has got what musical instrument? Write the names. There is one name that you don't need.*

Bruno Daniel Maria Patricia

clarinet drums flute

The two boys can each play two instruments.

The owner of the flute can play all three instruments.

The owner of the drums can only play one instrument.

The clarinet isn't Bruno's.

Maria can't play the clarinet.

# 4 SOLVE THE CODE. ARE THE SENTENCES TRUE FOR YOU?

| A | B | C | D | E | F | G | H | I |
|---|---|---|---|---|---|---|---|---|
| | O | | Q | | S | | U | |
| **J** | **K** | **L** | **M** | **N** | **O** | **P** | **Q** | **R** |
| W | | Y | | A | | C | | E |
| **S** | **T** | **U** | **V** | **W** | **X** | **Y** | **Z** | |
| | G | | I | | K | | M | |

**V guvax urnil zrgny vf gbb ybhq.**

I think heavy metal is too loud.

1 **V cersre snfg zhfvp, yvxr cbc.**

2 **Pbhagel zhfvp vf gbb fybj sbe zr.**

3 **V yvxr fybj, dhvrg pynffvpny zhfvp.**

## Words to learn

| Things to pack | | Around the world | |
|---|---|---|---|
| camera | ______ | Africa | ______ |
| guidebook | ______ | Antarctica | ______ |
| map | ______ | Arctic Ocean | ______ |
| matches | ______ | Asia | ______ |
| passport | ______ | Atlantic Ocean | ______ |
| sleeping bag | ______ | Caribbean Sea | ______ |
| suncream | ______ | Central America | ______ |
| sunglasses | ______ | Europe | ______ |
| swimsuit | ______ | Indian Ocean | ______ |
| tent | ______ | Mediterranean Sea | ______ |
| torch | ______ | North America | ______ |
| towel | ______ | Oceania | ______ |
| | | Pacific Ocean | ______ |
| | | South America | ______ |

## Phrases to learn

What are you going to do (this weekend)? ______

Do you want to come with (me / us)? ______

Sorry, I can't. ______

That sounds like fun! ______

I'd love to! ______

## 1 Which letters are missing from the alphabet? Put them in the correct order to see what the people are going to take on holiday.

B P J Q Y V I W
K U X L F Z O
G D S T H N

1 O X B W Z I Y
J L Q K G
T D P F H V

2 G B E Y M V F
Z K L X J I
D N P Q S U W A

3 N X A D P F Z
B G I K Q C V M
U S Y H J R

Hailey's going to take a *camera*.

1 Sam's not going to forget … .

2 Jake's going camping, so he needs a … .

3 Rita's going to take a … for her seaside holiday.

Unscramble the yellow letters to find what they are all going to take with them. Who do you think is going to take the thing in the green letters?

## 2 Put the letters in order. Write the names of the places.

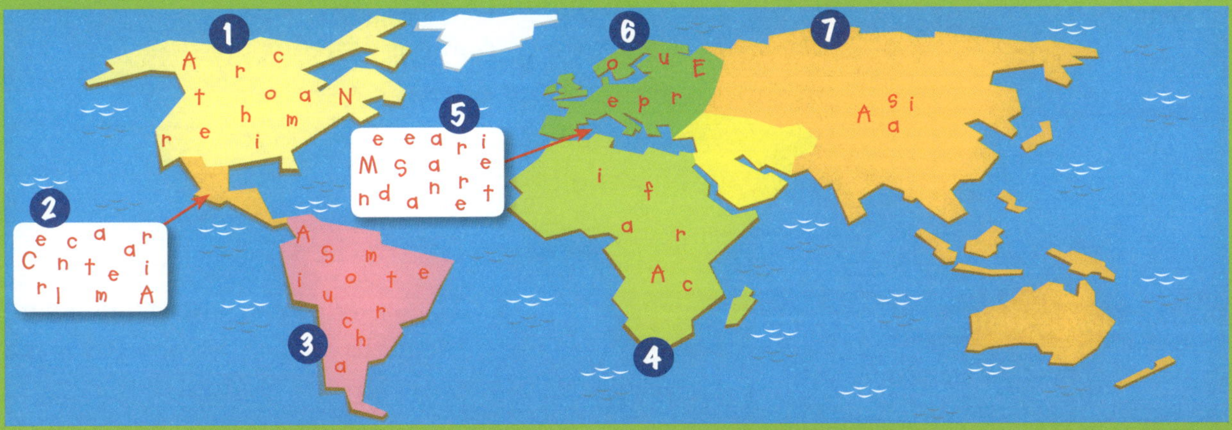


## 3 Follow the labyrinth. Find things to take on holiday.

| Start → | m | k | Finish |
|---|---|---|---|
| p | a | o | o |
| s | l | e | b |
| e | e | d | i |
| p | i | g | u |
| g | n | l | e |
| b | a | o | w |
| s | g | t | t |
| u | n | u | i |
| l | g | s | m |
| a | s | w | i |
| e | s | s | t |
| s | t | e | n |

Which of the things did you take on your last holiday?

## 4 Put the letters in order to find two places in each question.

fnpeiiceacncoaoaiac

*Pacific Ocean, Oceania*

1 baaberorinccinscacaetea

2 lananicacntatocarcteati

3 firnanaodcneicaia

Answers: see Teacher's Guide

## Describing your family

**1 Read the text.**

We use adjectives to talk about size, length and colour, and to give our opinions.

### My cousins

My cousins are cool! They're from Manchester, in the UK. My favourite cousin is Jamie. He's got long, fair hair and blue eyes.

Jamie's dad's name is Sam. He's got short, dark hair and brown eyes. His mum's name is Marie. She's got short, fair hair and blue eyes.

Jamie's got a big brother and two little sisters. His big brother's name is Fletcher. He's got short, dark hair and brown eyes. Their little sisters are Emily and Lucy. They've got long, dark hair and big, blue eyes.

opinion

length

colour

size

**Writing help** **Order of adjectives**

We put adjectives before nouns.

| | |
|---|---|
| little brother ✓ | brother little ✗ |

Adjectives don't change for different people.

| | |
|---|---|
| little brother ✓ | little sisters ✓ |
| little sister ✓ | littles sisters ✗ |

We can use two or more adjectives together. We put adjectives for size and length before adjectives for colour.

| | |
|---|---|
| big, blue eyes ✓ | blue, big eyes ✗ |

**2 Choose the correct options.**

My **best friend** / **friend best** is Justin. He's got (**1**) **fair, short** / **short, fair** hair and blue eyes. He's got two (**2**) **bigs** / **big** brothers and a (**3**) **little sister** / **sister little**.

His (**4**) **big brothers** / **brothers big** are Giles and Andrew. Giles has got long, dark hair and (**5**) **brown** / **browns** eyes. Andrew has got short, dark hair and (**6**) **blue eyes** / **eyes blue**.

Their sister Louisa has got long, fair hair and (**7**) **big, brown** / **brown, big** eyes.

**3 In your notebook, write about your best friend. Use adjectives and the writing guide.**

**My best friend**

My friends are ….

They're from ….

My best friend is ….

He's / She's got ….

**His / Her parents**

My friend's dad's name is ….

He's got ….

His mum's name is ….

She's got ….

**His / Her brothers and sisters**

My friend's got ….

….

## Describing a typical weekend

**1 Read the text.**

We use prepositions of time to say when we do things.

***on*** + days
+ parts of days

**My sister's weekend**

My sister Kylie plays a lot of sport at the weekend. On Saturday morning, she always goes swimming at nine o'clock. In the afternoon, she often plays tennis. In summer, I sometimes play too. In the evening, we watch DVDs or listen to music.

On Sunday, Kylie usually plays football. In winter, she always plays in a team. In June, July and August, she practises.

At one o'clock, we usually have Sunday lunch with my grandparents. In the afternoon and evening, we do our homework or we chat on the Internet with friends.

***at*** + times
+ the weekend

***in*** + the morning / the afternoon / the evening
+ months
+ seasons

***Writing help*** **Prepositions of time**

We use time expressions at the beginnings or the ends of sentences.

On Sunday, Kylie plays football. ✓

Kylie plays football on Sunday. ✓

Kylie plays on Sunday football. ✗

**2 Choose the correct options.**

We usually go shopping in **Saturday afternoons** / **(the afternoon)** / **three o'clock**.

1 I usually get up **in** / **on** / **(at)** seven o'clock **in** / **(on)** / **at** Mondays.

2 My brother often stays up late at **Saturday** / **(the weekend)** / **the evening**.

3 In **(winter)** / **Sunday afternoon** / **the weekend**, I never play sport.

4 We almost never **at the weekend go to the cinema** / **(go to the cinema at the weekend)** / **go at the weekend to the cinema**.

**3 In your notebook, write about the weekend activities of someone you know. Use the writing guide and at least six words or phrases from the box.**

| |
|---|
| in summer / winter   in the morning / afternoon |
| on Saturday / Sunday morning |
| at five o'clock / eight o'clock   at the weekend |
| always / usually / often / sometimes / never |

My … 's weekend

My … at the weekend.

On Saturday morning, he / she ….

In the afternoon, he / she ….

In the evening, ….

On Sunday, he / she ….

# Describing school life

**1 Read the text.**

We use capital letters for the first word of a sentence, the word *I*, the names of people and places, nationalities and languages, and days and months.

## My ideal school

I'm Kieran, and I'm Irish. I go to Saint Bernadette's School for boys in Dublin, Ireland. School's okay but I start classes very early and I finish classes very late, and my school subjects are boring. My ideal school is very different.

It's a school for boys and girls. We start classes late, at ten o'clock. On Fridays, we finish classes at lunch time.

We don't study history, geography or French. They're boring! We study art, English and music. English is easy. Art and music are interesting. I think my ideal school is fun!

the word *I*

names of people and places

nationalities and languages

first words of sentences

days and months

### *Writing help* Capital letters and starting sentences

We use a capital letter at the start of a sentence.

My ideal school is for boys and girls.

We use a full stop (.) or an exclamation mark (!) at the end of a sentence, but not at the start.

They're boring! ✓ ¡They're boring! ✗

We use a question mark (?) at the end of a question, but not at the start.

When do your classes start? ✓

¿When do your classes start? ✗

**2 Add capital letters to the paragraph.**

~~i'm~~ ~~alex~~ and ~~i'm~~ from ~~london~~, in ~~england~~. ~~at~~ my ideal school, ~~i~~ start classes late and ~~i~~ finish classes early. ~~my~~ friends and ~~i~~ study ~~spanish~~ and history but we don't study maths or science. ~~maths~~ and science are difficult! ~~what~~ do you think of my ideal school?

I'm
1 Alex
2 I'm
3 London
4 England
5 At
6 I
7 I
8 My
9 I
10 Spanish
11 Maths
12 What

**3 In your notebook, write about your ideal school. Use the writing guide.**

**Paragraph 1**
Your real school

**Paragraph 2**
Your ideal school

**Paragraph 3**
Subjects at your ideal school

## Describing a photo

**1 Read the text.**

Check your spelling for confusing words.

words with two vowels (a, e, i, o, u) next to each other

words that are like Spanish words

*-ing* forms

### My favourite photo

In my favourite photo, I'm with my friends. It's my birthday. It's warm and the sun is shining, so we're having a birthday picnic at the beach.

I'm sitting next to the water. I'm wearing a green T-shirt and jeans. My best friend, Darius, is behind me. He's wearing yellow shorts. My brother is next to Darius. He's wearing green shorts. My birthday cake is in front of me.

### *Writing help* Checking your spelling

Study what you write. Make a list of your spelling mistakes. Use your list to help you check your spelling.

| | |
|---|---|
| making ✓ | makeing ✗ |
| sitting ✓ | siting ✗ |
| photo ✓ | foto ✗ |
| goes ✓ | gos ✗ |
| friend ✓ | frend ✗ |

**2 Correct the spelling mistakes.**

In this ~~foto~~, my friend Carla is ~~shoping~~. She's ~~wering~~ her cool new jeans. She's ~~goeing~~ into her ~~favorit~~ shop. She's ~~lokking~~ at the ~~camara~~, and she's ~~smilling~~. She's very happy.

photo
1 shopping
2 wearing
3 going
4 favourite
5 looking
6 camera
7 smiling

**3 In your notebook, write about your favourite photo. Use the writing guide. Check your spelling.**

**Paragraph 1**
Who's in the photo?
What's the weather like?
What are the people doing?
Where are they?

**Paragraph 2**
Where's each person?
What's each person wearing?

# Describing a home

**1 Read the text.**

We use *and* to connect similar ideas and to make lists. We use *but* to contrast different ideas.

## *My ideal home*

*I live in a house in Oxford. I live there with my mum and my sister. Our home is beautiful but there isn't a bedroom for my sister. She shares my bedroom.*

*My ideal home is a flat. There's a bedroom for my mum, a bedroom for my sister, a bedroom for me and a bedroom for friends. There are four bathrooms and my bedroom has an en suite bathroom. The flat is very big and there's a living room, a dining room and a big kitchen. There isn't a garden but there's a balcony.*

contrast different ideas

make lists

connect similar ideas

### *Writing help* *and* and *but*

Connect your ideas to make long sentences.

**Similar ideas:** The room is big and it's got nice furniture.

**Make lists:** In my room, there's a bed, a desk, a chair and a wardrobe.

Connect your ideas to make your writing interesting.

I love our kitchen but I don't like our living room.

Our flat is nice but it's small.

**2 Complete the sentences. Use *and* or *but*.**

My parents want to buy a new flat, **but** I like our home.

1. My bedroom isn't very nice. It's small and ________ dark.
2. The furniture in this room is nice but ________ I don't like the colours.
3. In our kitchen, there's a fridge, a cooker, a cupboard and ________ a shelf.
4. I like my sister but ________ I don't want to share a room with her.
5. My bedroom is very big and ________ it's got three beds in it.

**3 In your notebook, write about your ideal home. Use the writing guide. Use *and* and *but* to connect your ideas.**

I live in a … in ….
I live there with ….
Our home is … but ….

My ideal home is ….
There's / There are ….
There isn't / There aren't ….

# Describing a restaurant

**1 Read the text.**

We use paragraphs to group our ideas when we write. We start a new paragraph when we change the subject.

This paragraph has got ideas about my ideal restaurant.

### My ideal restaurant

My favourite food is Italian food, so my ideal restaurant is an Italian restaurant. It's in Liverpool, next to my house, so I can eat there every day.

My ideal restaurant is famous for its pizzas but it also serves delicious pasta. It's got great beef and chicken dishes too, and the salads and vegetables are very good.

Of course, the desserts at my ideal restaurant are fantastic. They serve Italian ice cream, and they've got fifty different ice creams! I like chocolate ice cream but my favourite dessert is mango ice cream.

This paragraph has got ideas about main dishes at my ideal restaurant.

This paragraph has got ideas about desserts at my ideal restaurant.

**2 Circle the three paragraphs.**

There's an Indian restaurant next to my school called The Taj Mahal. Sometimes my family goes there at weekends. The Taj Mahal serves curry. There's beef curry, chicken curry, fish curry and vegetable curry. Curry isn't fantastic but it's okay. I think my favourite thing at The Taj Mahal is the Indian bread. It's called naan bread. You eat it with your curry. When we have a meal at the Taj Mahal, I always order naan bread with my curry.

**3 In your notebook, write about your ideal restaurant. Group your ideas in paragraphs. Use the writing guide to help you.**

**Paragraph 1**
Type of restaurant / food
Location

**Paragraph 2**
Main dishes

**Paragraph 3**
Desserts

# Describing a town

**1 Read the text.**

We use *also* and *too* to add extra information. We use *also* after *be* and before other main verbs. We use *too* at the ends of sentences.

at the end of a sentence

after be

before main verbs

Hi Damian,

How was your holiday? I was in Brighton with my cousins. It was fun, and the weather was great too.

Brighton is a town in the south of England, by the sea. It's got some fantastic shops. There are also lots of nice cafés and restaurants. My favourite place was the beach – you can sit by the sea and eat fish and chips. I also like the Royal Pavilion. It's like an Indian palace!

Where were you on holiday?

See you soon,

Pete

**2 Complete the sentences. Use *also* and *too*.**

There's a museum on Hurst Street. There's also an art gallery.

1 I really like Manchester. Liverpool is an interesting city too.

2 I love the shops in Edinburgh. I also think the restaurants are fantastic.

3 There are many large churches in Leeds. There's a cathedral too.

4 There's a good baker's in Walton Street. There's also a great cinema.

**3 In your notebook, write an email about a place you visited. Use the writing guide.**

Hi …,

How was your …?
I was in ….

… is in ….
It's got ….
My favourite place was ….

Where were you …?

See you soon,
…

## Writing a music report

**1 Read the text.**

When you write about a person's life, it's important to check that you use the correct tenses and the correct past forms.

irregular past forms

correct tense

### Beyoncé Knowles

Beyoncé Knowles is an American singer, actress and fashion model.

Beyoncé was born on 4th September 1981. Originally, she sang in the group Destiny's Child. Destiny's Child recorded four albums and sang songs for the films *Men in Black* and *Charlie's Angels*. In 2003, Beyoncé made her first solo album.

Between 2000 and 2009, Beyoncé made three albums, did three big world tours and acted in six films. She sold millions of records and won many music awards. Beyoncé is one of the most successful female singers in the world.

***Writing help*** **Checking your grammar**

Study what you write. Make a list of your grammar mistakes. Use your list to help you check your grammar.

Beyoncé acted in six films. ✓

Beyoncé acts in six films. ✗

**2 Correct the grammar mistakes.**

Beyoncé start her music career in the group Destiny's Child.

*Beyoncé started her music career in the group Destiny's Child.*

1 Beyoncé's hero music is Michael Jackson.
*Beyoncé's music hero is Michael Jackson.*

2 Beyoncé and rap star Jay Z was married on 4th April 2008.
*Beyoncé and rap star Jay Z were married on 4th April 2008.*

3 Beyoncé's rapper favourite is Wyclef Jean.
*Beyoncé's favourite rapper is Wyclef Jean.*

**3 Write about a singer or group that you like. Use the writing guide. Check your writing for grammar mistakes.**

**Paragraph 1**
Who?

**Paragraph 2**
Start of career

**Paragraph 3**
Career now

# Planning a holiday

**1 Read the text.**

We use sequence markers to show the order of events.

## My holiday plan

My name is Katya Endersby. I'm eighteen years old and I live in Liverpool. This summer I'm going to have a very special holiday. I'm going to work in the rainforest in Venezuela.

First, I'm going to fly to Caracas with my brother, Phil. We're going to spend a week in the city. Then we're going to travel to Santa Elena, and we're going to learn how to work in the rainforest.

After that, we're going to work in the rainforest for four weeks. We're going to clean up rubbish in the forest, and I want to help plant new trees too.

Finally, we're going to spend a week on the islands in the Caribbean Sea. I want to lie in the sun on the beach and go to a reggae concert in Jamaica!

That's the end of my special holiday.

### *Writing help* Sequence markers

Be careful with phrases that look the same but mean different things.

*first* → *the first thing I'm going to do*

First I'm going to Caracas. Then I'm going to Santa Elena.

*at first* → *for a short time, before a change*

At first he was kind but then he was horrible.

**2 Put the sentences in the correct order. Then complete the sentences. Use *first, then, after that* and *finally*.**

Then ________ I'm going to fly to Montelimar, in France, where the race begins. 3

After that ________, I'm going to cycle 172 km from Montelimar to Mont Ventoux. 4

In July, I'm going to cycle in the amateur group in a big bike race, the Tour de France. 1

Finally ________, I'm going to have a big party to celebrate! 5

First, I'm going to cycle every day with my new bike. 2

**3 In your notebook, write about your plans for next summer. Use the writing guide.**

**Paragraph 1**
My name is ….
This summer I'm going to ….

**Paragraph 2**
First, I'm going to ….
Then I'm / we're going to ….

**Paragraph 3**
After that, I'm / we're going to ….

**Paragraph 4**
Finally, I'm / we're going to ….
I want to ….

That's the end of my summer holiday.

| Vowels | | Consonants | |
|---|---|---|---|
| /i/ | happy | /p/ | pen |
| /ɪ/ | it | /b/ | big |
| /iː/ | he | /t/ | two |
| /æ/ | cat | /d/ | dog |
| /ɑː/ | art | /k/ | can |
| /e/ | egg | /g/ | good |
| /ɜː/ | girl | /tʃ/ | cheap |
| /ɒ/ | not | /dʒ/ | job |
| /ɔː/ | four | /f/ | food |
| /ʊ/ | look | /v/ | very |
| /uː/ | you | /θ/ | think |
| /ə/ | sugar | /ð/ | then |
| /ʌ/ | mum | /s/ | speak |
| /eɪ/ | day | /z/ | zoo |
| /aɪ/ | why | /ʃ/ | she |
| /ɔɪ/ | boy | /ʒ/ | television |
| /aʊ/ | how | /h/ | hat |
| /əʊ/ | go | /m/ | meat |
| /ɪə/ | ear | /n/ | now |
| /eə/ | wear | /ŋ/ | sing |
| /ʊə/ | tourist | /l/ | late |
| | | /r/ | red |
| | | /j/ | yes |
| | | /w/ | we |

# Unit 1

## Syllables

**1** 4.11 **Listen and repeat.**

adjective borrow daughter freckles grandfather hair Portugal twelfth wife

**2** **Write the words from exercise 1 in the correct columns.**

| One syllable | Two syllables | Three syllables |
|---|---|---|
| hair | borrow | adjective |
| twelfth | daughter | grandfather |
| wife | freckles | Portugal |

**3** 4.12 **Listen, check and repeat.**

# Unit 2

## Third person *-s*

**1** 4.13 **Listen. Circle the words you hear.**

talk / (talks)

1 speak / (speaks)
2 (chat) / chats
3 (read) / reads
4 study / (studies)
5 watch / (watches)
6 (do) / does

**2** 4.14 **Listen and repeat. Listen to the /s/, /z/ and /ɪz/ endings.**

| /s/ | /z/ | /ɪz/ |
|---|---|---|
| talks | reads | watches |

**3** 4.15 **Listen. Circle the final sounds you hear. Then listen, check and repeat.**

| | | | | |
|---|---|---|---|---|
| | plays | /s/ | (/z/) | /ɪz/ |
| 1 | thinks | (/s/) | /z/ | /ɪz/ |
| 2 | speaks | (/s/) | /z/ | /ɪz/ |
| 3 | sings | /s/ | (/z/) | /ɪz/ |
| 4 | teaches | /s/ | /z/ | (/ɪz/) |
| 5 | makes | (/s/) | /z/ | /ɪz/ |
| 6 | finishes | /s/ | /z/ | (/ɪz/) |
| 7 | studies | /s/ | (/z/) | /ɪz/ |
| 8 | lives | /s/ | (/z/) | /ɪz/ |
| 9 | uses | /s/ | /z/ | (/ɪz/) |

# Unit 3

## The sound /h/

**1** 4.16 **Listen and repeat.**

hair hand her hockey house

**2** 4.17 **Listen. Circle the words you hear.**

(hair) / air

1 his / (is)
2 hand / (and)
3 (how) / Ow!

**3** 4.18 **Listen and repeat.**

Who has got his homework?
He has dinner at home.
History homework is hard.
Harry and Heather are happy.

# Unit 4

## The sound /ŋ/

**1** 4.19 **Listen and repeat.**

chatting playing singing wearing

**2** 4.20 **Listen. Circle the words you hear.**

(rain in) / raining

1 go in / (going)
2 (thin) / thing
3 Ron / (wrong)

**3** 4.21 **Listen and repeat. Listen to the /ŋ/ sound.**

I'm listening to my favourite song.
He's buying something.
We're doing the writing exercise.
It's six o'clock in the morning and you're watching TV!

# Unit 5

## Word stress

**1** 4.22 **Listen and repeat. How many syllables have the words got? Write 2 or 3.**

kitchen 2
1 balcony 3
2 dinner 2
3 computer 3
4 comfortable 3
5 enormous 3
6 wardrobe 2
7 aerobics 3
8 patio 3
9 mirror 2
10 Chinese 2
11 today 2

**2** 4.23 **Listen and repeat.**

| ●• | •● | ●•• | •●• |
|---|---|---|---|
| garden | Japan | balcony | computer |

**3** 4.24 **Listen to the words from exercise 1 again. Write the words in the correct columns.**

| ●• | •● |
|---|---|
| kitchen | Chinese |
| dinner | today |
| wardrobe | |
| mirror | |
| **●••** | **•●•** |
| balcony | computer |
| comfortable | enormous |
| patio | aerobics |

# Unit 6

## Sentence stress and rhythm

**1** 4.25 **Listen and repeat. Stress the red words.**

I've got some eggs.

I don't like jam or honey.

**2** 4.26 **Listen and repeat. Underline the stressed words in each sentence.**

Tom wants some toast.

1 We can make a pizza.
2 He's cooking dinner.
3 Put it in the fridge.
4 Is the cooker hot?
5 Mary isn't having dinner.

# Unit 7

## Intonation in questions

**1** 4.27 **Listen to the intonation in the questions.**

**Rising ↗**

Was it hot?

Do you like it?

Are you listening?

**Falling ↘**

Where were you?

What are you doing?

How often do you play?

**2** 4.28 **Listen to the sentences. Does the intonation rise or fall? Write ↗ or ↘.**

Was there a party? ↗

1 What was that song? ↘
2 Is it raining? ↗
3 Were they good? ↗
4 How do I get there? ↘
5 Where are you going? ↘
6 Have you got a pen? ↗

# Unit 8

## Past simple endings

**1** 4.29 **Listen and repeat. Notice the -*ed* sounds at the ends of the verbs.**

| /d/ | /t/ | /ɪd/ |
|---|---|---|
| loved | stopped | wanted |

**2** 4.30 **Listen. Circle the correct -*ed* sounds. Then, listen, check and repeat.**

| | | | |
|---|---|---|---|
| | danced | (/t/) | /ɪd/ |
| 1 | composed | (/d/) | /ɪd/ |
| 2 | wanted | /t/ | (/ɪd/) |
| 3 | planned | (/d/) | /ɪd/ |
| 4 | recorded | /d/ | (/ɪd/) |
| 5 | asked | (/t/) | /ɪd/ |

# Unit 9

## Weak forms: *must* and *can*

**1** 4.31 **Listen and repeat.**

**Unstressed**

You must stop.

I can play.

Can you understand?

**Stressed**

You mustn't go.

I can't speak French.

Yes, I can.

No, I can't.

**2** 4.32 **Listen. Are the red words stressed or unstressed? Write S or U.**

They mustn't run. S

1 Can you play tennis? U
2 You can come to my party. U
3 Yes, we can. S
4 We must leave now. U
5 I can't do this exercise. S

## A

a /ə/ un, una
accident /'æksɪdənt/ accidente
acrobatics /ækrə'bætɪks/ acrobacias
(cycle) across /'saɪkl ə'krɒs/ cruzar (en bici)
activity /æk'tɪvəti/ actividad
actor /'æktə/ actor
actress /'æktrəs/ actriz
adventure /'ədventʃə/ aventura
aerobics /eə'rəʊbiks/ aerobic
aeroplane /'eərəpleɪn/ avión
Africa /'æfrɪkə/ África
after /'ɑ:ftə/ después de
after that /ɑ:ftə 'ðæt/ después de eso
afternoon /ɑ:ftə'nu:n/ tarde
(in the) afternoon /ɪn ði ɑftə'nu:n/ (por la) tarde
after-school activity /ɑ:ftəsku:l æk'tɪvəti/ actividad extraescolar
again /ə'gen, ə'geɪn/ otra vez
airport /'eəpɔ:t/ aeropuerto
album /'ælbəm/ disco
algebra /'ældʒɪbrə/ álgebra
all /ɔ:l/ todos
all the time /ɔ:l ðə 'taɪm/ todo el tiempo
almost never /ɔ:lməʊst 'nevə/ casi nunca
alone /ə'ləʊn/ solo
also /'ɔ:lsəʊ/ también
always /'ɔ:lweɪʒ/ siempre
American /ə'merɪkən/ americano
an /ən/ un, una
and /ænd/ y
animal /'ænɪml/ animal
another /ə'nʌðə/ otro
Antarctica /æn'tɑ:ktɪkə/ Antártida
antique /æn'ti:k/ antigüedad
any /'eni/ algún, ningún, nada de
anyone /'eniwʌn/ alguien, nadie
anything /'eniθɪŋ/ algo, nada
apple /'æpl/ manzana
apple juice /'æpl dʒu:s/ zumo de manzana
April /'eɪprəl/ abril
aquarium /ə'kweəriəm/ acuario
architect /'ɑ:kɪtekt/ arquitecto, arquitecta
Arctic Ocean /ɑ:ktɪk 'əʊsn/ Océano Ártico
area /'eəriə/ área, zona
argue /'ɑ:gju:/ discutir
arm /ɑ:m/ brazo
armchair /'ɑ:mtʃeə/ sillón
around /ə'raʊnd/ del, alrededor de
arrive /ə'raɪv/ llegar
arrive back /əraɪv 'bæk/ volver
art /ɑ:t/ plástica
art gallery /'ɑ:t gæləri/ galería de arte
artist /'ɑ:tɪst/ artista
Asia /'eɪʃə: 'eɪʒə/ Asia
ask /ɑ:sk/ preguntar
asleep /ə'sli:p/ dormido
assemble /ə'sembl/ montar
at all /ət 'ɔ:l/ en absoluto, para nada
at home /ət 'həʊm/ en casa
athletics /æθ'letɪks/ atletismo
Atlantic Ocean /ætlæntɪk 'əʊʃn/ Océano Atlántico
atlas /'ætləs/ atlas
attraction /ə'trækʃn/ atracción
audience /'ɔ:diəns/ público
August /'ɔ:gəst/ agosto
aunt /ɑ:nt/ tía
autumn /'ɔ:təm/ otoño
award /ə'wɔ:d/ premio

## B

baby /'beɪbi/ bebé
bacon /'beɪkən/ beicon, bacón
bad /bæd/ malo
bag /bæg/ bolsa
baked beans /beɪkt 'bi:nz/ judías en salsa de tomate
baker's /'beɪkəz/ panadería
balcony /'bælkəni/ balcón
ball /bɔ:l/ pelota
banana /bə'nɑ:nə/ plátano
band /bænd/ grupo de música
barbecue /'bɑ:bɪkju:/ barbacoa
baseball /'beɪsbɔ:l/ béisbol
baseball cap /beɪsbɔ:l 'kæp/ gorra de béisbol
basic /'beɪsɪk/ básico
basketball /'bɑ:skɪtbɔ:l/ baloncesto
bath /bɑ:θ/ bañera
bathroom /'bɑ:θru:m, 'bɑ:θrʊm/ cuarto de baño
be /bi:/ ser, estar
be born /bi 'bɔ:n/ nacer
be called /bi 'kɔ:ld/ llamarse
be careful /bi 'keəfl/ tener cuidado
beach /bi:tʃ/ playa
beautiful /'bju:tɪfl/ precioso
because /bɪ'kɒz, bɪ'kəz/ porque
become /bɪ'kʌm/ hacerse
bed /bed/ cama
bedroom /'bedru:m, 'bedrʊm/ habitación, dormitorio
bedside table /bedsaɪd 'teɪbl/ mesilla
before /bɪ'fɔ:/ antes (de)
behind /bɪ'haɪnd/ detrás (de)
bell /bel/ campana
best /best/ (el) mejor
best friend /best 'frend/ (el) mejor amigo, mejor amiga
big /bɪg/ grande
bike /baɪk/ bici
billion /'bɪljən/ mil millones
biology /baɪ'ɒlədʒi/ biología
bird /bɜ:d/ pájaro
birthday /'bɜ:θdaɪ/ cumpleaños
biscuit /'bɪskɪt/ galleta
black /blæk/ negro
block of flats /blɒk əv 'flæts/ bloque de pisos
blue /blu:/ azul
blues (music) /blu:z/ (música de) blues
board /bɔ:d/ tablón de anuncios
boarder /'bɔ:də/ alumno interno, alumna interna
boarding school /'bɔ:dɪŋ sku:l/ internado
boat /bəʊt/ barco
body /'bɒdi/ cuerpo
book /bʊk/ libro
bookcase /'bʊkkeɪs/ estantería
boots /bu:ts/ botas
bored /bɔ:d/ aburrido
boring /'bɔ:rɪŋ/ aburrido, que aburre
borrow /'bɒrəʊ/ tomar prestado
box /bɒks/ caja
boy /bɔɪ/ chico
boy band /'bɔɪ bænd/ grupo de música de chicos
Brazil /brə'zɪl/ Brasil
bread /bred/ pan
break /breɪk/ descanso, recreo
break up /breɪk 'ʌp/ separarse
breakfast /'brekfəst/ desayuno
bridge /brɪdʒ/ puente
bright /braɪt/ fuerte
brightly /'braɪtli/ brillante
brilliant /'brɪliənt/ genial
bring /brɪŋ/ traer
British /'brɪtɪʃ/ británico
brother /'brʌðə/ hermano
brown /braʊn/ marrón
building /'bɪldɪŋ/ edificio
bungalow /'bʌŋgələʊ/ bungalow, casa de una altura
bus /bʌs/ autobús
bus station /'bʌs steɪʃn/ estación de autobuses
bus stop /'bʌs stɒp/ parada del autobús
busy /'bɪzi/ ocupado
but /bʌt/ pero
butter /'bʌtə/ mantequilla
buy /baɪ/ comprar

## C

cab /kæb/ taxi
café /'kæfeɪ/ cafetería
cake /keɪk/ tarta
call /kɔ:l/ llamar
call back /kɔ:l 'bæk/ devolver una llamada
camera /'kæmərə/ cámara
can /kæn/ poder
can't /kɑ:nt/ no poder
Canada /'kænədə/ Canadá
Canadian /kə'neɪdiən/ canadiense
canteen /kæn'ti:n/ comedor escolar
cap /kæp/ gorra
capital /'kæpɪtl/ capital
car /kɑ:/ coche
cardboard /'kɑ:dbɔ:d/ cartón
career /kə'rɪə/ trayectoria profesional
Caribbean /kærɪ'bi:ən, kə'rɪbiən/ Caribe
Caribbean Sea /kærɪbi:ən 'si:, kərɪbiən 'si:/ Mar Caribe
carnival /'kɑ:nɪvl/ carnaval
carrot /'kærət/ zanahoria
carry /'kæri/ llevar / desplazar
cartoon /kɑ:'tu:n/ dibujos animados
castle /'kɑ:sl/ castillo
casual /'kæʒuəl/ informal
cat /kæt/ gato
catch /kætʃ/ coger
cathedral /kə'θi:drəl/ catedral
CD player /si:'di: pleɪə/ reproductor de CDs
celebrate /'selɪbreɪt/ celebrar
cello /'tʃeləʊ/ violonchelo, chelo
Central America /sentrəl ə'merɪkə/ América Central
cereal /'sɪəriəl/ cereal(es)
chair /tʃeə/ mesa
champion /'tʃæmpiən/ campeón, campeona
change /tʃeɪndʒ/ cambio, cambiar
charts /tʃɑ:ts/ listas
chat /tʃæt/ charlar, chatear
chat on the Internet /tʃæt ɒn ði 'ɪntənet/ chatear en Internet
cheap /tʃi:p/ barato
cheese /tʃi:z/ queso
cheeseburger /'tʃi:zbɜ:gə/ hamburguesa con queso
chemist's /'kemɪsts/ farmacia
chest of drawers /tʃest əv 'drɔ:z/ cómoda
chicken /'tʃɪkɪn/ pollo
child /tʃaɪld/ niño, niña
children /'tʃɪldrən/ niños, niñas
China /'tʃaɪnə/ China
Chinese /tʃaɪ'ni:z/ chino
chips /tʃɪps/ patatas fritas
chocolate /'tʃɒklət/ chocolate
chocolate cake /'tʃɒklət keɪk/ tarta de chocolate
church /tʃɜ:tʃ/ iglesia
cinema /'sɪnəmə/ cine
circle /'sɜ:kl/ círculo
city /'sɪti/ ciudad
claim /kleɪm/ decir, afirmar
clap /klæp/ aplaudir
clarinet /klærɪ'net/ clarinete
class /klɑ:s/ clase
classical (music) /'klæsɪkl/ (música) clásica
classmate /'klɑ:smeɪt/ compañero, compañera de clase
classroom /'klɑ:sru:m, 'klɑ:srʊm/ clase, aula
climb /klaɪm/ subir a
clock /klɒk/ reloj
close /kləʊz/ cerrar
closed /kləʊzd/ cerrado
clothes /kləʊdz, kləʊz/ ropa
clothes shop /'kləʊðz ʃɒp, 'kləʊz ʃɒp/ tienda de ropa
cloud /klaʊd/ nube
cloudy /'klaʊdi/ nublado
club /klʌb/ club, grupo
coast /kəʊst/ costa
coat /kəʊt/ abrigo, chaquetón
coffee /'kɒfi/ café
cola /'kəʊlə/ cola
cold /kəʊld/ frío
collect /kə'lekt/ coleccionar
collection /kə'lekʃn/ colección
colour /'kʌlə/ color
colourful /'kʌləfl/ lleno de color

combination /kɒmbɪ'neɪʃn/ combinación
combine /kəm'baɪn/ combinar
come /kʌm/ venir
come in /kʌm 'ɪn/ entrar en
comedy programme /'kɒmədi prəʊgræm/ programa cómico
comfortable /'kʌmftəbl/ cómodo
comic /'kɒmɪk/ cómico, humorista
common /'kɒmən/ frecuente, normal
compare /kəm'peə/ comparar
compete /kəm'pi:t/ competir
competition /kɒmpə'tɪʃn/ concurso
complete /kəm'pli:t/ completo
complicated /'kɒmplɪkeɪtɪd/ complicado
compose /kəm'pəʊz/ componer
composer /kəm'pəʊzə/ compositor, compositora
computer /kəm'pju:tə/ ordenador
concert /'kɒnsət/ concierto
concert hall /'kɒnsət hɔ:l/ sala de conciertos
conditions /kən'dɪʃnz/ condiciones
connect /kə'nekt/ conectar(se)
connected /kə'nektɪd/ conectado
construct /kən'strʌkt/ construir, montar
contest /'kɒntest/ festival, certamen
continent /'kɒntɪnənt/ continente
continue /kən'tɪnju:/ seguir
convert /kən'vɜ:t/ transformar
cook /kʊk/ cocinar
cooker /'kʊkə/ cocina
cool /ku:l/ guay, actual
copy /'kɒpi/ copiar
corner /'kɔ:nə/ esquina
correct /kə'rekt/ correcto
costume /'kɒstju:m/ traje
cottage /'kɒtɪdʒ/ casita (de campo)
cotton /'kɒtn/ algodón
counter /'kaʊntə/ barra, mostrador
country /'kʌntri/ país
country (music) /'kʌntri/ (música) country
cousin /'kʌzn/ primo, prima
crazy /'kreɪzi/ chiflado
crisps /krɪsps/ patatas fritas de bolsa
cross /krɒs/ cruzar
crossword puzzle /'krɒswɜ:d pʌzl/ crucigrama
cultural /'kʌltʃərəl/ cultural
culture /'kʌltʃə/ cultura
cupboard /'kʌbəd/ armario
curry /'kʌri/ curry
customer /'kʌstəmə/ cliente, clienta
cute /kju:t/ guapo, mono
cycle /'saɪkl/ andar en bici
cycling /'saɪklɪŋ/ andar en bici
cyclist /'saɪklɪst/ ciclista
cymbals /'sɪmblz/ platillos

## D

dad /dæd/ padre, papá
dance /dɑ:ns/ bailar
dance music /'dɑ:ns mju:zɪk/ música de baile
dancing /'dɑ:nsɪŋ/ baile
dark /dɑ:k/ oscuro
date /deɪt/ fecha
daughter /'dɔ:tə/ hija
day /deɪ/ día
December /dɪ'sembə/ diciembre
decide /dɪ'saɪd/ decidir
delicious /dɪ'lɪʃəs/ delicioso
dentist /'dentɪst/ dentista
design /dɪ'zaɪn/ diseño
designer /dɪ'zaɪnə/ diseñador, diseñadora
desk /desk/ mesa, escritorio
dessert /dɪ'zɜ:t/ postre
detached /dɪ'tætʃt/ (casa) individual, no adosada
dictionary /'dɪkʃənri/ diccionario
die /daɪ/ morir
different /'dɪfrənt/ diferente
difficult /'dɪfɪkəlt/ difícil
diner /'daɪnə/ cafetería (típica americana)
dining room /'daɪnɪŋ ru:m, daɪnɪŋ rʊm/ comedor
dinner /'dɪnə/ cena
dinosaur /'daɪnəsɔ:/ dinosaurio
directions /də'rekʃnz, dɪ'rekʃnz, daɪ'rekʃnz/ indicaciones
disc /dɪsk/ disco
dislike /dɪs'laɪk/ desagradar, no gustar
distinctive /dɪstɪŋktɪv/ marcado, distintivo
diva /'di:və/ diva
do /du:/ hacer
do homework /du: 'həʊmwɜ:k/ hacer los deberes
do karate /du: kə'rɑ:ti/ hacer kárate
do puzzles /du: 'pʌzlz/ hacer puzzles
documentary film /dɒkju'mentri fɪlm/ documental
dog /dɒg/ perro
don't worry /dəʊnt 'wʌri/ no te preocupes
doner kebab /dɒnə kɪ'bæb/ kebab
dormitory /'dɔ:mɪtri/ dormitorio común
double-decker /dʌbl 'dekə/ de dos pisos
drama /'drɑ:mə/ teatro
draw /drɔ:/ dibujar
drawer /drɔ:/ cajón
dream /dri:m/ sueño
dress /dres/ vestido
drink /drɪŋk/ beber
drums /drʌmz/ batería
during /'djʊərɪŋ/ durante

## E

ear /ɪə/ oreja
early /ɜ:li/ temprano
east /i:st/ este
easy /'i:zi/ fácil
eat /i:t/ comer
egg /eg/ huevo
Egyptian /i'dʒɪpʃn/ egipcio
eight /eɪt/ ocho
eighteen /eɪ'ti:n/ dieciocho
eighth /eɪtθ/ octavo
eighty /'eɪti/ ochenta
elaborate /ɪ'læbərət/ elaborado
elephant /'elɪfənt/ elefante
eleven /ɪ'levn/ once
eleventh /ɪ'levənθ/ undécimo
email /'i:meɪl/ email
emblem /'embləm/ emblema, insignia
encyclopedia /ensaɪklə'pi:diə/ enciclopedia
end /end/ final
English /'ɪŋglɪʃ/ (de) inglés
enormous /ɪ'nɔ:məs/ enorme
enter /'entə/ pasar
equipment /ɪ'kwɪpmənt/ material
especially /ɪ'speʃəli/ especialmente, sobre todo
Europe /'jʊərəp/ Europa
evening /'i:vnɪŋ/ tarde-noche
(in the) evening /'i:vnɪŋ/ (por la) tarde-noche
every /'evri/ todos los
everybody /'evribɒdi/ todo el mundo
everyone /'evriwʌn/ toda la gente
everything /'evriθɪŋ/ todo
exam /ɪg'zæm/ examen
example /ɪg'zɑ:mpl/ ejemplo
excellent /'eksələnt/ excelente
exciting /ɪk'saɪtɪŋ/ emocionante
excuse me /ɪk'skju:z mi:/ perdón
exercise /'eksəsaɪz/ ejercicio
exhibit /ɪg'zɪbɪt/ objeto en exposición
expensive /ɪk'spensɪv/ caro
experience /ɪk'spɪəriəns/ experiencia
experiment /ɪk'sperɪmənt/ experimento
extra /'ekstrə/ adicional
eye /aɪ/ ojo

## F

face /feɪs/ cara
fair /feə/ claro, rubio
false /fɒls/ falso
family /'fæməli/ familia
family tree /fæməli 'tri:/ árbol genealógico
famous /'feɪməs/ famoso
fan /fæn/ aficionado, aficionada
fantastic /fæn'tæstɪk/ fantástico
fantasy /'fæntəsi/ de fantasía
fashionable /'fæʃnəbl/ elegante
fast /fɑ:st/ rápido
fast food /fɑ:st 'fu:d/ comida rápida
fat /fæt/ grasa
father /'fɑ:ðə/ padre
fatty /'fæti/ graso
favourite /'feɪvərɪt/ favorito
February /'februəri/ febrero
feel /fi:l/ sentir, notar
festival /'festɪvl/ festival
fifteen /fɪf'ti:n/ quince
fifth /fɪfθ/ quinto
fifty /'fɪfti/ cincuenta
fill /fɪl/ llenar
film /fɪlm/ película
film star /'fɪlm stɑ:/ estrella de cine
finally /'faɪnəli/ al final
finish /'fɪnɪʃ/ acabar
finish classes /fɪnɪʃ 'klɑ:səz/ acabar las clases
fire /'faɪə/ fuego
first /fɜ:st/ primero
fish /fɪʃ/ pez (peces), pescado
five /faɪv/ cinco
flag /flæg/ bandera
flamenco /flə'menkəʊ/ flamenco
flat /flæt/ piso, apartamento
floor /flɔ:/ piso, altura
flower /'flaʊə/ flor
flute /flu:t/ flauta (travesera)
fly /flaɪ/ ondear
foggy /'fɒgi/ (haber) niebla
food /fu:d/ comida
foot /fʊt/ pie
football /'fʊtbɔ:l/ fútbol
football player /'fʊtbɔ:l pleɪə/ jugador, jugadora de fútbol
footballer /'fʊtbɔ:lə/ futbolista
for /fɔ:/ por, durante
for example /fər ɪg'zɑ:mpl/ por ejemplo
forget /fə'get/ olvidar
form /fɔ:m/ medio
form /fɔ:m/ crear, formar
forty /'fɔ:ti/ cuarenta
four /fɔ:/ cuatro
four o'clock /fɔ:r ə'klɒk/ las cuatro
fourteen /fɔ:'ti:n/ catorce
fourth /fɔ:θ/ cuarto
France /frɑ:ns/ Francia
fraternal /frə'tɜ:nl/ mellizos
freckles /'freklz/ pecas
free /fri:/ gratis
free time /fri: 'taɪm/ tiempo libre
free-time activity /fri: taɪm æk'tɪvəti/ actividad de tiempo libre
French /frenʃ/ francés
Friday /'fraɪdeɪ/ viernes
fridge /frɪdʒ/ frigorífico
fried (fish) /fraɪd/ (pescado) frito
friend /frend/ amigo, amiga
from /frɒm/ de
fruit /fru:t/ fruta
fruit salad /fru:t 'sæləd/ macedonia de frutas
full /fʊl/ completo
fun /fʌn/ divertido, entretenido, diversión
funny /'fʌni/ gracioso
furniture /'fɜ:nɪtʃə/ muebles

## G

game /geɪm/ juego
garage /'gærɑ:ʒ, 'gærɑ:dʒ, 'gærɪdʒ/ garaje
garden /'gɑ:dn/ jardín
general /'dʒenrəl/ general
genius /'dʒi:niəs/ genio
geography /dʒi'ɒgrəfi/ geografía
geology /dʒi'ɒlədʒi/ geología
geometry /dʒi'ɒmətri/ geometría
German /'dʒɜ:mən/ alemán
get around /get ə'raʊnd/ moverse por
get dressed /get 'drest/ vestirse
get started /get 'stɑ:tɪd/ empezar

get up /get 'ʌp/ levantarse
get wet /get 'wet/ mojarse
girl /gɜ:l/ chica
girlfriend /'gɜ:lfrend/ novia
give /gɪv/ dar
glasses /'glɑsəz/ gafas
go /gəʊ/ ir
go camping /gəʊ 'kæmpɪŋ/ ir de camping
go home /gəʊ 'həʊm/ irse a casa
go shopping /gəʊ 'ʃɒpɪŋ/ ir de compras
go skateboarding /gəʊ 'skeɪtbɔ:dɪŋ/ practicar skate
go snorkelling /gəʊ 'snɔ:kəlɪŋ/ bucear
go to bed /gəʊ tə 'bed/ acostarse
go to the cinema /gəʊ tə ðə 'sɪnəmə/ ir al cine
good /gʊd/ bueno
good at /'gʊd æt/ bueno en
Good idea! /gʊd aɪ'dɪə/ ¡Qué buena idea!
gospel (music) /'gɒspl/ gospel, (músical) espiritual
grandfather /'grænfɑ:ðə/ abuelo
grandma /'grænmɑ:/ abuela
grandmother /'grænmʌðə/ abuela
grandpa /'grænpɑ:/ abuelo
grandparents /'grænpeərənts/ abuelos
great /greɪt/ genial
Greece /gri:s/ Grecia
Greek /gri:k/ griego
green /gri:n/ verde
green salad /gri:n 'sæləd/ ensalada de lechuga
ground floor /graʊnd 'flɔ:/ planta baja
group /gru:p/ grupo
guidebook /'gaɪdbʊk/ guía
guitar /gɪ'tɑ:/ guitarra
gymnastics /dʒɪm'næstiks/ gimnasia

## H

hair /heə/ pelo
half past /'hɑ:f pɑ:st/ y media
halfway /hɑ:f'weɪ, 'hɑ:fweɪ/ hasta la mitad
hall /hɔ:l/ hall, entrada
hamburger /'hæmbɜ:gə/ hamburguesa
hand /hænd/ mano
happy /'hæpi/ contento, feliz
harp /hɑ:p/ harpa
hat /hæt/ sombrero
hate /heit/ odiar
have /hæv/ tener
have a break /hæv ə 'breɪk/ tomarse un descanso, hacer una pausa
have a shower /hæv ə 'ʃaʊə/ darse una ducha
have breakfast /hæv 'brekfəst/ desayunar
have dinner /hæv 'dɪnə/ cenar
have got /hæv 'gɒt/ tener
have lunch /hæv 'lʌntʃ/ comer (a mediodía)
he /hi:/ él
head /hed/ cabeza
hear /hɪə/ oír
hear (of) /hɪə/ oír (hablar de)
heartbreak /'hɑ:tbreɪk/ sufrimiento, congoja
heavy metal /hevi 'metl/ heavy metal
hello /he'ləʊ/ hola
help /help/ ayudar
her /hɜ:/ (llamar)la
here /hɪə/ aquí
Hi! /haɪ/ ¡Hola!
him hɪm/ (conocer)lo
hip hop (music) /'hɪp hɒp/ hip hop
his /hɪz/ su, sus
historic /hɪ'stɒrɪk/ histórico
history /'hɪstri/ historia
hit /hɪt/ golpear
hit /hɪt/ éxito
hockey /'hɒki/ hockey
holiday /'hɒlɪdeɪ/ vacaciones
homepage /'həʊmpeɪdʒ/ página principal
honey /'hʌni/ miel
hope /həʊp/ esperar
horoscope /'hɒrəskəʊp/ horóscopo
hospital /'hɒspɪtl/ hospital
hot /hɒt/ (hacer) calor
hot dog /'hɒt dɒg/ perrito caliente
hotel /həʊ'tel/ hotel
hour /'aʊə/ hora
house /haʊs/ casa
how long? /haʊ 'lɒŋ/ ¿cuánto tiempo?
how many? /haʊ 'meni/ ¿cuántos?
how much? /haʊ 'mʌtʃ/ ¿cuánto?
how often? /haʊ 'ɒfn, haʊ 'ɒftən/ ¿con qué frecuencia?
how tall? /haʊ 'tɔ:l/ ¿qué altura?
human /'hju:mən/ humano
hundred /'hʌndrəd/ cien
hungry /'hʌŋgri/ (tener) hambre
husband /'hʌzbənd/ marido

## I

I /aɪ/ yo
ice cream /aɪs 'kri:m, 'aɪs kri:m/ helado
ice hockey /'aɪs hɒki/ patinaje sobre hielo
ice rink /'aɪs rɪŋk/ pista de patinaje
ice skating /'aɪs skeɪtɪŋ/ patinaje sobre hielo
icon /'aɪkɒn/ icono
ICT /aɪsi:'ti:/ TIC
icy /'aɪsi/ helado
identical /aɪ'dentɪkl/ idéntico
if /ɪf/ si
imitate /'ɪmɪteɪt/ imitar
immigrant /'ɪmɪgrənt/ inmigrante
important /ɪm'pɔ:tənt/ importante
impressive /ɪm'presɪv/ impresionante
in /ɪn/ en
in front of /ɪn 'frʌnt ɒv/ delante de
in love /ɪn 'lʌv/ enamorado
include /ɪn'klu:d/ incluir
incredible /ɪn'kredɪbl/ increíble
independent /ɪndɪ'pendənt/ independiente
India /'ɪndiə/ India
Indian /'ɪndiən/ indio
Indian Ocean /ɪndiən 'əʊʃn/ Océano Índico
indoor /'ɪndɔ:/ (deportes) de pista
indoors /ɪn'dɔ:z/ en pista
information /ɪnfə'meɪʃn/ información
insect /'ɪnsekt/ insecto
inside /ɪn'saɪd/ dentro
instead /ɪn'sted/ en lugar de eso
instructor /ɪn'strʌktə/ monitor, monitora
instrument /'ɪnstrəmənt/ instrumento
interesting /'ɪntrəstɪŋ/ interesante
international /ɪntə'næʃnəl/ internacional
internationally /ɪntə'næʃnəli/ en el ámbito internacional
invitation /ɪnvɪ'teɪʃn/ invitación
invite /ɪn'vaɪt/ invitar
Ireland /'aɪələnd/ Irlanda
island /'aɪlənd/ isla
it /ɪt/ él, ella (objeto o animal)
it's cloudy /ɪts 'klaʊdi/ está nublado
it's cold /ɪts 'kəʊld/ hace frío
it's cool /ɪts 'ku:l/ hace fresco
it's foggy /ɪts 'fɒgi/ hay niebla
it's hot /ɪts 'hɒt/ hace calor
it's icy /ɪts 'aɪsi/ está helado
it's rainy /ɪts 'reɪni/ está lloviendo
it's snowy /ɪts 'snəʊi/ está nevando
it's stormy /ɪts 'stɔ:mi/ hay tormenta
it's sunny /ɪts 'sʌni/ hace sol
it's warm /ɪts 'wɔ:m/ hace calor
it's windy /ɪts 'wɪndi/ hace viento
Italian /ɪ'tæliən/ italiano
Italy /'ɪtəli/ Italia
its /ɪts/ su, sus (de un objeto o animal)

## J

jacket /'dʒækɪt/ chaqueta
jam /dʒæm/ mermelada
January /'dʒænjuəri/ enero
Japan /dʒə'pæn/ Japón
Japanese /dʒæpə'ni:z/ japonés
jazz /dʒæz/ jazz
jeans /dʒi:nz/ pantalones vaqueros
join /dʒɔɪn/ unirse a
juice /dʒu:s/ zumo
July /dʒu'laɪ/ julio
jump /dʒʌmp/ saltar
jumper /'dʒʌmpə/ jersey
June /dʒu:n/ junio

## K

keep cool /ki:p 'ku:l/ mantener fresco
ketchup /'ketʃəp/ ketchup
keyboard /'ki:bɔ:d/ teclado
kilogram /'kɪləgræm/ kilogramo
kilometre /'kɪləmi:tə, kɪ'lɒmɪtə/ kilómetro
king /kɪŋ/ rey
kiss /kɪs/ besar
kitchen /'kɪtʃɪn/ cocina
know /nəʊ/ conocer

## L

laboratory /lə'bɒrətri/ laboratorio
lamp /læmp/ lámpara
landmark /'lændmɑ:k/ edificio, monumento famoso
language /'læŋgwɪdʒ/ lengua, idioma
large /lɑ:dʒ/ grande
last /lɑ:st/ último
last /lɑ:st/ durar
last (year) /lɑ:st/ (el año) pasado
late /leɪt/ tarde
later /'leɪtə/ después, más tarde
laughter /'lɑ:ftə/ risa
league /li:g/ liga
learn /lɜ:n/ aprender
leather /'leðə/ piel, cuero
leave /li:v/ salir de (casa)
leave home /li:v 'həʊm/ salir de casa
left /left/ (girar) a la izquierda
leg /leg/ pierna
lesson /'lesn/ clase
let /let/ dejar
let's go /lets 'gəʊ/ vamos
letter /'letə/ carta
library /'laɪbrəri/ biblioteca
life /laɪf/ vida
light /laɪt/ luz
like /laɪk/ gustar
like /laɪk/ como
line /laɪn/ línea
list /lɪst/ lista
listen /'lɪsn/ escuchar (música)
listen to music /lɪsn tə 'mju:zɪk/ escuchar música
little /'lɪtl/ pequeño
a little /ə 'lɪtl/ un poco
live /lɪv/ vivir
living room /'lɪvɪŋ ru:m, 'lɪvɪŋ rʊm/ sala de estar
location /ləʊ'keɪʃn/ ubicación
long /lɒŋ/ largo, de largo, durar...
look /lʊk/ mirar, sentar/no sentar bien, estilo
look for /'lʊk fɔ:/ buscar
lots of /'lɒts əv/ muchos
loud /laʊd/ ruidoso, alto
loudly /'laʊdli/ a gran volumen
love /lʌv/ encantar
Lucky you! /lʌki 'ju:/ ¡Qué suerte tienes!
lunch /lʌntʃ/ comida (al mediodía)
lunchtime /'lʌntʃtaɪm/ hora de comer

## M

magazine /mægə'zi:n/ revista
magic /'mædʒɪk/ magia
main dish /meɪn 'dɪʃ/ plato fuerte
make /meɪk/ hacer
make models /meɪk 'mɒdlz/ construir maquetas

make the bed /meɪk ðə 'bed/ hacer la cama
man /mæn/ hombre
many /'meni/ muchos
map /mæp/ mapa
March /mɑːtʃ/ marzo
market /'mɑːkɪt/ mercado
marry /'mæri/ casarse (con)
martial arts /mɑːʃl 'ɑːts/ artes marciales
master /'mɑːstə/ dueño, dueña
match /mætʃ/ partido
matches /'mætʃɪz/ cerillas
material /mə'tɪəriəl/ tejido
maths /mæθs/ matemáticas
May /meɪ/ mayo
maybe /'meɪbi/ quizá
mayonnaise /meɪə'neɪz/ mahonesa
meal /miːl/ comida
mean /miːn/ significar
medicine /'medsn, 'medɪsn/ medicina(s)
medieval /medi'iːvl/ medieval
Mediterranean Sea /medɪtəreɪniən 'siː/ Mar Mediterráneo
meet /miːt/ quedar con (amigos)
meet friends /miːt 'frendz/ quedar con amigos
member /'membə/ miembro
mention /'menʃn/ mencionar
menu /'menjuː/ carta
message /'mesɪdʒ/ mensaje
metal /'metl/ (de) metal
metre /'miːtə/ metro
middle /'mɪdl/ (en) medio
middle /'mɪdl/ parte central
milk /mɪlk/ leche
million /'mɪljən/ millón
minute /'mɪnɪt/ minuto
mirror /'mɪrə/ espejo
miss /mɪs/ echar de menos
mobile phone /məʊbaɪl 'fəʊn/ teléfono móvil
model /'mɒdl/ maqueta
modern /'mɒdn/ moderno
(at the) moment /'məʊmənt/ (en este) momento
Monday /'mʌndeɪ/ lunes
month /mʌnθ/ mes
more /mɔː/ más
(in the) morning /'mɔːnɪŋ/ (por la) mañana
most /məʊst/ (el) más
mother /'mʌðə/ madre
motocross /'məʊtəʊkrɒs/ motocross
mountain /'maʊntən/ montaña
mountain range /'maʊntən reɪndʒ/ cordillera
mouth /maʊθ/ boca
move /muːv/ trasladarse
move house /muːv 'haʊs/ cambiar de casa
movie /'muːvi/ película
MP3 player /empiː'θriː pleɪə/ reproductor de MP3
much /mʌtʃ/ mucho
mum /mʌm/ madre, mamá
mummy /'mʌmi/ mamá
museum /mju'ziːəm/ museo
mushy peas /mʌʃi 'piːz/ guisantes reblandecidos
music /'mjuːzɪk/ música
music shop /'mjuːzɪk ʃɒp/ tienda de música
musical /'mjuːzɪkl/ musical
musician /mju'zɪʃn/ músico
must /mʌst/ deber
my /maɪ/ mi, mis

## N

name /neɪm/ nombre
named /neɪmd/ llamado
national /'næʃnəl/ nacional
nationality /næʃə'næləti/ nacionalidad
natural /'nætʃrəl/ natural
near /nɪə/ cerca de
nearby /nɪə'baɪ/ cerca
need /niːd/ necesitar
neon /'niːɒn/ neón
net /net/ red
never /'nevə/ nunca
new /njuː/ nuevo
news /njuːz/ noticias
next /nekst/ siguiente
next to /'nekst tuː/ junto a
next (week) /nekst/ (la semana) que viene
nice /naɪs/ bonito
nickname /'nɪkneɪm/ apodo
night /naɪt/ noche
nine /naɪn/ nueve
nineteen /naɪn'tiːn/ diecinueve
ninety /'naɪnti/ noventa
ninth /naɪnθ/ noveno
no one /'nəʊ wʌn/ nadie
no problem /'nəʊ prɒbləm/ ningún problema
No way! /'nəʊ weɪ/ ¡Ni hablar!
noise /nɔɪz/ ruido
non-stop /nɒn'stɒp/ sin parar
north /nɔːθ/ norte
North America /nɔːθ ə'merɪkə/ Norteamérica
North Pole /nɔːθ 'pəʊl/ Polo Norte
Northern Ireland /nɔːðən 'aɪələnd/ Irlanda del Norte
nose /nəʊz/ nariz
not only… /nɒt 'əʊnli/ no solo…
notebook /'nəʊtbʊk/ cuaderno
novel /'nɒvl/ novela
November /nəʊ'vembə/ noviembre
now /naʊ/ ahora
number /'nʌmbə/ número

## O

object /'ɒbdʒekt/ objeto
Oceania /əʊʃi'ɑːniə/ Oceanía
October /ɒk'təʊbə/ octubre
of course /əv 'kɔːs/ por supuesto
official /ə'fɪʃl/ oficial
officially /ə'fɪʃəli/ oficialmente
often /'ɒfn, 'ɒftən/ a menudo
OK /əʊ'keɪ/ vale
old /əʊld/ viejo
on /ɒn/ en
on time /ɒn 'taɪm/ a tiempo
one /wʌn/ uno
only /'əʊnli/ solo
open /'əʊpən/ abierto
open /'əʊpən/ abrir
opera /'ɒprə/ ópera
opinion /ə'pɪnjən/ opinión
opposite /'ɒpəzɪt/ opuesto, contrario
option /'ɒpʃn/ opción
or /ɔː/ o
orange /'ɒrɪndʒ/ naranja
orange juice /'ɒrɪndʒ dʒuːs/ zumo de naranja
orchestra /'ɔːkestrə/ orquesta
order /'ɔːdə/ pedir, orden, apuntar lo que pide el cliente
origin /'ɒrɪdʒɪn/ origen
originally /ə'rɪdʒənəli/ originalmente
other /'ʌðə/ otros
our /ɑː/ nuestro, nuestros
outdoor /'aʊtdɔː/ al aire libre
outside /aʊt'saɪd/ fuera
over /'əʊvə/ por encima de
own /əʊn/ propio

## P

Pacific Ocean /pəsɪfɪk 'əʊʃn/ Océano Pacífico
pack a bag /pæk ə 'bæg/ hacer la maleta
package /'pækɪdʒ/ paquete
page /peɪdʒ/ página
paint /peɪnt/ pintar
painting /'peɪntɪŋ/ cuadro
(in) pairs /peəz/ (por) parejas
palace /'pæləs/ palacio
paper /'peɪpə/ periódico
parade /pə'reɪd/ desfile
parents /'peərənts/ padres
park /pɑːk/ parque
part /pɑːt/ parte
party /'pɑːti/ fiesta
pass /pɑːs/ pasar, aprobar
passenger /'pæsɪndʒə/ viajero, viajera
passion /'pæʃn/ pasión
passport /'pɑːspɔːt/ pasaporte
pasta /'pæstə/ pasta
patio /'pætiəʊ/ terraza, patio
pay /peɪ/ pagar
PE /piː'iː/ Educación Física
peanut butter /piːnʌt 'bʌtə/ pasta de cacahuete
peas /piːz/ guisantes
pedestrian crossing /pədestriən 'krɒsɪŋ/ paso de zebra
pen /pen/ bolígrafo
pence /pens/ peniques
pencil /'pensl/ lápiz
pencil case /'pensl keɪs/ estuche
penguin /'peŋgwɪn/ pingüino
people /'piːpl/ gente
per cent /pə 'sent/ por ciento
percentage /pə'sentɪdʒ/ porcentaje
percussion instrument /pə'kʌʃn ɪnstrəmənt/ instrumento de percusión
perfect /'pɜːfekt/ perfecto
permission /pə'mɪʃn/ permiso
person /'pɜːsn/ persona
pets /pets/ mascotas
phone /fəʊn/ teléfono
phone number /'fəʊn nʌmbə/ número de teléfono
photo /'fəʊtəʊ/ foto
photographer /fə'tɒgrəfə/ fotógrafo, fotógrafa
picnic /'pɪknɪk/ picnic, comida al aire libre
picture /'pɪktʃə/ dibujo
piece /piːs/ pieza, obra
pink /pɪŋk/ rosa
place /pleɪs/ sitio, lugar
plan /plæn/ planear, planificar
plant /plɑːnt/ planta
plastic /'plæstɪk/ (de) plástico
play /pleɪ/ jugar a, tocar (un instrumento)
play computer games /pleɪ kəm'pjuːtə geɪmz/ jugar con juegos de ordenador
play football /pleɪ 'fʊtbɔːl/ jugar al fútbol
play the piano /pleɪ ðə pi'ænəʊ/ tocar el piano
player /'pleɪə/ jugador, jugadora
please /pliːz/ por favor
police officer /pə'liːs ɒfɪsə/ (agente de) policía
police station /pə'liːs steɪʃn/ comisaría (de policía)
polo shirt /'pəʊləʊ ʃɜːt/ polo
pool /puːl/ piscina
pop (music) /pɒp/ (música) pop
popular /'pɒpjələ/ popular, famoso
population /pɒpju'leɪʃn/ población
portion /'pɔːʃn/ ración
Portugal /'pɔːtʃʊgl/ Portugal
Portuguese /pɔːtʃʊ'giːz/ portugués
post office /'pəʊst ɒfɪs/ (oficina de) correos
postcard /'pəʊstkɑːd/ postal
potato /pə'teɪtəʊ/ patata
pound /paʊnd/ libra
pour /pɔː/ verter, servir
practise /'præktɪs/ practicar, ensayar
prefer /prɪ'fɜː/ preferir
prepare /prɪ'peə/ preparar
present /'preznt/ regalo
pretend /prɪ'tend/ fingir
pretty /'prɪti/ bonito
primary /'praɪməri/ (de) primaria
prince /prɪns/ príncipe
private /'praɪvət/ privado
private school /praɪvət 'skuːl/ escuela privada
probably /'prɒbəbli/ probablemente
professional /prə'feʃənl/ profesional
profile /'prəʊfaɪl/ perfil
(TV) programme /'prəʊgræm/ programa (de televisión)
protect yourself /prə'tekt jəself/ protegerte
protective /prə'tektɪv/ protector
public /'pʌblɪk/ público

purple /'pɜ:pl/ morado
put /pʊt/ poner, dejar
put back /pʊt 'bæk/ volver a poner, dejar
put on /pʊt 'ɒn/ encender
puzzle /'pʌzl/ puzzle
pyramid /'pɪrəmɪd/ pirámide

## Q

quarter past /kwɔ:tə' pɑ:st/ y cuarto
quarter to /kwɔ:tə 'tu:/ menos cuarto
queen /kwi:n/ reina
quiet /'kwaɪət/ callado

## R

rain /reɪn/ llover
raincoat /'reɪnkəʊt/ gabardina
rainforest /'reɪnfɒrəst/ selva tropical
rainy /'reɪni/ lluvioso
raise /reɪz/ levantar
rap (music) /ræp/ (música) rap
reach /ri:tʃ/ alcanzar
read magazines /ri:d mægə'zi:nz/ leer (revistas)
real /rɪəl/ real
really /'rɪəli/ realmente, muy
Really? /'rɪəli/ ¿De verdad?
record /rɪ'kɔ:d/ grabar
red /red/ rojo
reggae /'regeɪ/ reggae
region /'ri:dʒən/ región
regularly /'regjələli/ con regularidad
relax /rɪ'laks/ relajarse
remember /rɪ'membə/ recordar
report /rɪ'pɔ:t/ informe, ficha
residence /'rezɪdəns/ residencia
restaurant /'restrɒnt/ restaurante
retro /'retrəʊ/ retro
return /rɪ'tɜ:n/ volver
rice /raɪs/ arroz
right /raɪt/ adecuado
right /raɪt/ (girar) a la derecha
river /'rɪvə/ río
roast beef /rəʊst 'bi:f/ rosbif
rock /rɒk/ roca, piedra
rock (music) /rɒk/ (música) rock
rock and roll /rɒk n 'rəʊl/ rock and roll
Roman /'rəʊmən/ romano
roof /ru:f/ tejado
room /ru:m/ or /rʊm/ habitación
routine /ru:'ti:n/ hábito
row /rəʊ/ hilera, remar
rowing /'rəʊɪŋ/ remo
royal /'rɔɪəl/ real
rubber /'rʌbə/ goma
rugby /'rʌgbi/ rugby
ruins /'rʊ:ɪnz/ ruinas, restos
rule /ru:l/ norma
ruler /'ru:lə/ regla
Russia /'rʌʃə/ Rusia

## S

safe /seɪf/ seguro
sale /seɪl/ rebajas
salsa /'sælsə/ salsa (estilo de baile)
salt /sɔ:lt, sɒlt/ sal
same /seɪm/ mismo
sandals /'sændlz/ sandalias
sandwich /'sændwɪtʃ/ sandwich
Saturday /'sætədeɪ/ sábado
sauce /sɔ:s/ salsa
sausage /'sɒsɪdʒ/ salchicha
saxophone /'sæksəfəʊn/ saxofón
say /seɪ/ decir
scarf /skɑ:f/ bufanda, pañuelo
school /sku:l/ escuela, instituto, (la vida) en la escuela
science /'saɪəns/ ciencias
Scotland /'skɒtlənd/ Escocia
Scottish /'skɒtɪʃ/ escocés
sea /si:/ mar
season /'si:zn/ estación
second /'sekənd/ segundo
section /'sekʃn/ sección
see (a film) /si:/ ver (una película)
semi-detached /semidɪ'tætʃt/ (vivienda) adosada en un lado
send /send/ enviar
separate /'seprət/ distinto
September /sep'tembə/ septiembre
serve /sɜ:v/ servir
serving /'sɜ:vɪŋ/ ración
seven /'sevn/ siete
seventeen /sevn'ti:n/ diecisiete
seventh /'sevnθ/ séptimo
seventy /'sevnti/ setenta
sex /seks/ sexo
shake /ʃeɪk/ agitar
share /ʃeə/ compartir
she /ʃi:/ ella
shelf /ʃelf/ balda, estante
shine /ʃaɪn/ brillar
shirt /ʃɜ:t/ camisa
shoe /ʃu:/ zapato
shop /ʃɒp/ tienda
shop assistant /'ʃɒp əsɪstənt/ dependiente, dependienta
shopping centre /'ʃɒpɪŋ sentə/ centro comercial
short /ʃɔ:t/ corto
shorts /ʃɔ:ts/ pantalones cortos
shower /'ʃaʊə/ ducha
side /saɪd/ lado
side dish /'saɪd dɪʃ/ guarnición, acompañamiento
silence /'saɪləns/ silencio
similar /'sɪmɪlə/ similar
simple /'sɪmpl/ simple
sing /sɪŋ/ cantar
singer /'sɪŋə/ cantante
sink /sɪŋk/ lavabo
sister /'sɪstə/ hermana
sit /sɪt/ sentarse
six /sɪks/ seis
sixteen /sɪks'ti:n/ dieciséis
sixth /sɪksθ/ sexto
sixty /'sɪksti/ sesenta
skiing /'ski:ɪŋ/ esquí
skirt /skɜ:t/ falda
sleep /sli:p/ dormir
sleeping bag /'sli:pɪŋ bæg/ saco de dormir
slice /slaɪs/ rodaja
slide rule /'slaɪd ru:l/ regla de cálculo
slow /sləʊ/ lento
small /smɔ:l/ pequeño
smart /smɑ:t/ elegante
smell /smel/ oler
smoothie /'smu:ði/ mezcla de zumo y batido
snow /snəʊ/ nevar
snowy /'snəʊi/ nevando
so /səʊ/ así es que
sock /sɒk/ calcetín
sofa /'səʊfə/ sofá
soft /sɒft/ blando
some /sʌm/ algunos
someone /'sʌmwʌn/ alguien
something /'sʌmθɪŋ/ algo
sometimes /'sʌmtaɪmz/ a veces
son /sʌn/ hijo
song /sɒŋ/ canción
soon /su:n/ pronto
sorry /'sɒri/ perdón
soul (music) /səʊl/ (música) soul
south /saʊθ/ sur
South America /saʊθ ə'merɪkə/ Sudamérica
southern hemisphere /ʃvðən 'hemɪsfɪə/ hemisferio sur
spaghetti /spə'geti/ espaguetis
Spain /speɪn/ España
Spanish /'spænɪʃ/ español
speak /spi:k/ hablar
special /'speʃl/ especial
spectator /spek'teɪtə/ espectador, espectadora
spend /spend/ pasar (tiempo), gastar (dinero)
sport /spɔ:t/ deporte
sports centre /'spɔ:ts sentə/ polideportivo
sporty /'spɔ:ti/ deportista
spring /sprɪŋ/ primavera
stadium /'steɪdiəm/ estadio
stairs /steəz/ escaleras
stall /stɔ:l/ puesto
stamps /stæmps/ sello
stand /stænd/ estar de pie
stand up /stænd 'ʌp/ ponerse de pie
star /stɑ:/ protagonizar
(pop) star /stɑ:/ estrella (del pop)
start classes /stɑ:t 'klɑ:sɪz/ empezar (las clases)
state school /'steɪt sku:l/ escuela pública
statue /'stætju:/ estatua
stay (in a hotel) /steɪ/ alojarse (en un hotel)
stool /stu:l/ taburete, banqueta
stop /stɒp/ parar
stormy /'stɔ:mi/ tormentoso
story /'stɔ:ri/ historia
straight /streɪt/ recto
straight /streɪt/ directamente
straight on /streɪt'ɒn/ todo recto
strawberry /'strɔ:bəri/ fresa
street /stri:t/ calle
string instrument /'strɪŋ ɪnstrəmənt/ instrumento de cuerda
strong /strɒŋ/ fuerte
student /'stju:dnt/ estudiante
studio /'stju:diəʊ/ estudio
study /'stʌdi/ estudiar
style /staɪl/ estilo
subject /'sʌbdʒekt/ asignatura
submarine /'sʌbməri:n/ submarino
such /sʌtʃ/ tan
sudoku puzzle /su'dəʊku: pʌzl/ sudoku
summer /'sʌmə/ verano
suncream /'sʌnkri:m/ crema solar
Sunday /'sʌndeɪ/ domingo
sunglasses /'sʌnglɑ:sɪz/ gafas de sol
sunny /'svni/ soleado
superhero /'su:pəhɪərəʊ/ superhéroe
supermarket /'su:pəmɑ:kɪt/ supermercado
surf /sɜ:f/ hacer surf
surface /'sɜ:fɪs/ superficie
surname /'sɜ:neɪm/ apellido
swim /swɪm/ nadar
swimming /'swɪmɪŋ/ natación
swimming pool /'swɪmɪŋ pu:l/ piscina
swimsuit /'swɪmsu:t/ bañador
symphony /'sɪmfəni/ sinfonía
system /'sɪstəm/ sistema

## T

table /'teɪbl/ mesa
take /teɪk/ coger (el autobús)
take /teɪk/ llevar (tiempo)
Take a look! /teɪk ə 'lʊk/ ¡Echa un vistazo!
take an exam /teɪk ən ɪg'ʒæm/ hacer un examen
take away /teɪk ə'weɪ/ llevar
take the bus /teɪk ð 'bʌs/ coger el autobús
take turns /teɪk 'tɜ:nz/ turnarse
takeaway food /'teɪkəweɪ fu:d/ comida para llevar
talent /'tælənt/ talento
talent contest /'tælənt kɒntest/ concurso de nuevos talentos
talk on the phone /tɔ:k ɒn ðə 'fəʊn/ hablar (por teléfono)
tall /tɔ:l/ alto, de altura
tambourine /tæmbə'ri:n/ tambor
tea /ti:/ té, merienda
teach /ti:tʃ/ enseñar
teacher /'ti:tʃə/ profesor, profesora
team /ti:m/ (de) equipo
technology /tek'nɒlədʒi/ tecnología
teenager /'ti:neɪdʒə/ joven, adolescente
teeth /ti:θ/ dientes
television /'telɪvɪʒn/ televisión
tell /tel/ decir, contar
tell the time /tel ðə 'taɪm/ decir la hora
ten /ten/ diez
tennis /'tenɪs/ tenis
tennis player /'tenɪs pleɪə/ jugador, jugadora de tenis
tennis racquet /'tenɪs rækɪt/ raqueta de tenis

tent /tent/ tienda de campaña
tenth /tenθ/ décimo
terraced (house) /'terəst/ (vivienda) adosada
terrible /'terɪbl/ horrible
test /test/ test, examen
text /tekst/ texto
textbook /'tekstbʊk/ libro de texto
that /ðæt/ ese, eso, aquel, aquello
the UK /ðə juː'keɪ/ el Reino Unido
the United Kingdom /ðə juːnaɪtɪd 'kɪŋdəm/ el Reino Unido
the USA /ðə juːes'eɪ/ los EEUU
theatre /'θɪətə/ teatro
their /ðeə/ su, sus
theme park /'θiːm pɑːk/ parque temático
then /ðen/ entonces, después
there /ðeə/ ahí, allí
there are /ðeər 'ɑː/ hay
there is /ðeər ɪz/ hay
these /ðiːz/ estos
they /ðeɪ/ ellos, ellas
thing /θɪŋ/ cosa
think /θɪŋk/ parecer
third /θɜːd/ tercero
thirteen /θɜː'tiːn/ trece
thirty /'θɜːti/ treinta
this /ðɪs/ este
those /ðəʊz/ esos, aquellos
thousand /'θaʊzənd/ mil
three /θriː/ tres
through /θruː/ a lo largo de
throw /θrəʊ/ lanzar
Thursday /'θɜːzdeɪ/ jueves
ticket /'tɪkɪt/ entrada
tie /taɪ/ corbata
till /tɪl/ caja (registradora)
time /taɪm/ tiempo, vez
timetable /'taɪmteɪbl/ horario
title /'taɪtl/ título
toast /təʊst/ tostada(s)
today /tə'deɪ/ hoy
together /tə'geðə/ juntos, a la vez
toilet /'tɔɪlət/ baño
tomato /tə'mɑːtəʊ/ tomate
tonight /tə'naɪt/ esta noche
tonne /tʌn/ tonelada
too /tuː/ también
top /tɒp/ (de) arriba
topping /'tɒpɪŋ/ condimento, relleno
torch /tɔːtʃ/ linterna
total /'təʊtl/ total
touch /tʌtʃ/ tocar
tour /tʊə, 'tɔː/ visita, recorrido
tourist /'tʊərɪst, 'tɔːrɪst/ turista
towel /'taʊəl/ toalla
tower block /'taʊə blɒk/ bloque alto, torre de apartamentos
town /taʊn/ ciudad
tracksuit /'træksuːt/ chándal
tracksuit top /'træksuːt tɒp/ chaqueta de chándal
tradition /trə'dɪʃn/ tradición
traditional /trə'dɪʃənl/ tradicional
traffic light /'træfɪk laɪt/ semáforo
train /treɪn/ tren
train station /'treɪn steɪʃn/ estación del ferrocarril
trainers /'treɪnəz/ zapatillas de deporte
transport /'trɑːnspɔːt/ transporte
travel /'trævl/ viajar
triangle /'traɪæŋgl/ triángulo
trigonometry /trɪgə'nɒmətri/ trigonometría
trip /trɪp/ viaje
trombone /trɒm'bəʊn/ trombón
trousers /'traʊzəz/ pantalones
true /truː/ verdadero
trumpet /'trʌmpɪt/ trompeta
try /traɪ/ intentar
T-shirt /'tiːʃɜːt/ camiseta de manga corta
tuba /'tjuːbə/ tuba
Tuesday /'tjuːzdeɪ/ martes
turn /tɜːn/ girar (a la izquierda/ derecha)
turn off /tɜːn 'ɒf/ apagar
TV show /tiː'viː ʃəʊ/ progama de televisión
twelfth /twelfθ/ duodécimo
twelve /twelv/ doce
twenty /'twenti/ veinte
twin /twɪn/ mellizo
twist /twɪst/ bailar twist
two /tuː/ dos
type /taɪp/ tipo
typical /'tɪpɪkl/ típico
typically /'tɪpɪkli/ suele

## U

umbrella /ʌm'brelə/ paraguas
uncle /'ʌŋkl/ tío
under /'ʌndə/ bajo, debajo de
underground (system) /'ʌndəgraʊnd/ (sistema de) metro
uniform /'juːnɪfɔːm/ uniforme
unusual /ʌn'juːʒuəl, ʌn'juːʒəl/ poco común, extraño
us /ʌs/ nos
use /juːz/ utilizar
usually /'juːʒuəli: 'juːʒəli/ generalmente

## V

vase /vɑːz/ jarrón
version /'vɜːʒn/ versión
very /'veri/ muy
video /'vɪdiəʊ/ vídeo
view /vjuː/ vista
village /'vɪlɪdʒ/ pueblecito
vinegar /'vɪnɪgə/ vinagre
violin /vaɪə'lɪn/ violín
visit /'vɪzɪt/ visitar
visitor /'vɪzɪtə/ visitante
volleyball /'vɒlibɔːl/ voleibo

## W

wait /weɪt/ esperar
waitress /'weɪtrəs/ camarera
Wales /weɪlz/ Gales
wall /wɔːl/ pared
want /wɒnt/ querer
wardrobe /'wɔːdrəʊb/ armario (ropero)
warm /wɔːm/ caliente
warm up /wɔːm 'ʌp/ calentar
watch TV /wɒtʃ tiː'viː/ ver (la tele)
water /'wɔːtə/ agua
water polo /'wɔːtə pəʊləʊ/ waterpolo
water tower /'wɔːtə taʊə/ torre de suministro de agua
way /weɪ/ dirección, distancia
we /wiː/ nosotros, nosotras
wear /weə/ llevar puesto, vestir
weather /'weðə/ tiempo meteorológico
Wednesday /'wenzdeɪ, 'wenzdi/ miércoles
week /wiːk/ semana
weekday /'wiːkdeɪ/ día de la semana
weekend /'wiːkend/ fin de semana
weigh /weɪ/ pesar
well /wel/ bueno
west /west/ oeste
wet /wet/ mojarse
What a shame! /wɒt ə 'ʃeɪm/ ¡Qué pena!
what? /wɒt/ ¿qué?
what's (the weather) like? /wɒts ðə 'weðə laɪk/ ¿qué (tiempo) hace?
when /wen/ cuando
when? /wen/ ¿cuándo?
where /weə/ donde
where? /weə/ ¿dónde?
which /wɪtʃ/ que
which? /wɪtʃ/ ¿qué? ¿cuál?
while /waɪl/ mientras
white /waɪt/ blanco
whiteboard /'waɪtbɔːd/ pizarra
who? /huː/ ¿quién?
whole /həʊl/ todo
why? /waɪ/ ¿por qué?
wife /waɪf/ mujer, esposa
win /wɪn/ ganar
wind instrument /'wɪnd ɪnstrəmənt/ instrumento de viento
window /'wɪndəʊ/ ventana
windsurfing /'wɪndsɜːfɪŋ/ windsurf
windy /'wɪndi/ (hacer) viento
winter /'wɪntə/ invierno
with /wɪð: wɪθ/ con
without /wɪ'ðaʊt/ sin
woman /'wʊmən/ mujer
wonder /'wʌndə/ preguntarse
wonderful /'wʌndəfl/ maravilloso
wool /wʊl/ lana
work /wɜːk/ trabajar
world /wɜːld/ mundo
world record /wɜːld 'rekɔːd/ récord mundial
worried /'wʌrid/ preocupado
worry /'wʌri/ preocupación
Wow! /waʊ/ ¡Vaya!
write /raɪt/ escribir

## X

xylophone /'zaɪləfəʊn/ xilófono

## Y

year /jɪə/ año
yellow /'jeləʊ/ amarillo
yesterday /'jestədeɪ/ ayer
yogurt /'jɒgət/ yogur
you /juː/ tú, usted, vosotros, vosotras, ustedes
young /jʌŋ/ joven
your /jɔː/ tu, tus, su, sus

# Expression Bank

|  |  |
|---|---|
| After that ... | Después ...<br>A continuación ... |
| And to drink? | ¿Y para beber? |
| Anything else? | ¿Alguna otra cosa? |
| Bye! | ¡Adiós! |
| Can I borrow it? | ¿Puedo toimarlo prestado? |
| Can I help you? | ¿Puedo ayudarte? |
| Can I speak to ...? | ¿Puedo hablar con ...? |
| Can I take your order? | ¿Puedo tomar nota? |
| Can you call back? | ¿Puedes vover a llamar? |
| Do you want to ...? | ¿Te apetece ...? |
| Excuse me | Disculpa |
| Finally | Finalmente |
| First ... | En primer lugar ... |
| Goodbye | Adiós |
| Good idea! | ¡Buena idea! |
| Go straight on | Sigue recto |
| Great! | ¡Genial! |
| Hello! | ¡Hola! |
| Here's your change | Aquí tienes el cambio |
| Here you are | Aquí tienes |
| Hi! | ¡Hola! |
| Hi, it's Paul | Hola, soy Paul |
| How are you? | ¿Cómo estás? |
| How do I get there? | ¿Cómo llego allí? |
| How much is this? | ¿Cuánto cuesta esto? |
| I'd like ... | Me gustaría ...<br>Yo tomaría ... |
| I'd love to | Me encantaría |
| I hope ... | Espero que ... |
| I'm fine | Estoy bien |
| I'm from Chicago | Soy de Chicago |
| I'm not very good at ... | No se me da muy bien ... |
| I'm sorry | Lo siento |
| It's cloudy | Está nublado |
| It's cold | Hace frío |
| It's cool | Hace fresco |
| It's fantastic! | ¡Es fantástico! |
| It's foggy | Hay niebla |
| It's fun! | ¡Qué divertido! |
| It's half past six | Son las seis y media |
| It's hot | Hace calor |
| It's icy | Hace mucho frío (hiela) |
| It's quarter past six | Son las seis y cuarto |
| It's quarter to six | Son las seis menos cuarto |
| It's rainy | Llueve |
| It's six o'clock | Son las seis en punto |
| It's snowy | Nieva |
| It's stormy | Hay tormenta |
| It's sunny | Hace sol |
| It's warm | Hace calor |
| It's windy | Hace viento |
| Let's ... | ¿Por qué no ...? |
| Look! | ¡Mira! |
| Me too | Yo también |
| My name's ... | Me llamo ... |
| Nice to meet you | Encantado de conocerte |
| Of course | Por supuesto |
| Oh, really? | ¿De verdad? |
| OK | Vale |
| See you there | Nos vemos allí |
| Shall we ...? | Podríamos ... |
| Sorry! | ¡Perdón! |
| Thanks! | ¡Gracias! |
| Thank you! | ¡Gracias! |
| That's great! | ¡Es genial! |
| Turn left | Gira a la izquierda |
| Turn right | Gira a la derecha |
| Welcome | Bienvenido/a |
| What time is it? | ¿Qué hora es? |
| Where are you from? | ¿De dónde eres? |
| Why don't we ...? | ¿Por qué no ...? |
| Wow! | ¡Caramba!<br>¡Vaya! |
| You're welcome | De nada.<br>No hay de qué. |